Edwin Arlington Robinson

Selected Early Poems

and Letters

EDITED BY CHARLES T. DAVIS

Princeton University

Holt, Rinehart and Winston

NEW YORK • CHICAGO • SAN FRANCISCO

TORONTO • LONDON

Third Printing, January, 1964

Copyright © 1960 by Holt, Rinehart and Winston, Inc.
Library of Congress Catalog Card Number: 60-15097
21752-0110
Printed in the United States of America

TO

Eve and Gay Allen

ꙮ ꙮ ꙮ

Contents

CAPTAIN CRAIG: A BOOK OF POEMS

LETTERS

❦ ❦ ❦

INTRODUCTION

I. E. A. ROBINSON AND THE CRAFT
OF THE MODERN POET

It is easy to say that modern American poetry begins with Edwin Arlington Robinson. His first published volumes, *The Torrent and The Night Before* (1896) and *The Children of the Night* (1897), which are reprinted in their entirety in this book, precede by more than a decade the writing, the talking, the organizing of energetic pioneers and front-runners like Harriet Monroe, Ezra Pound, and Amy Lowell. Robinson's accomplishment remains impressive, even when we view it from the perspective of more than a half century of growth in the literary arts. While living still in the nineteenth century, Robinson developed a poetic technique which broke away clearly from Victorian practice and a poetic intelligence which, if not thoroughly in harmony with the preoccupations of Pound, or Eliot, or Sandburg, sought as well to face the serious intellectual problems of his time and not to discover comforting refuge in the precious dream worlds of much late nineteenth-century verse.

How was Robinson's technique "modern"? For one thing, it rejected the language of the "poetical," which consisted largely of the outworn conventions and mannerisms of romantic diction when Robinson began to write. The poets of the new century were determined to use real speech, to capture the nuances of the living language, and not to compromise with old habits by applying the often exotic devices of the waning Romantic impulse. These might be suggestions of the archaic through the imitation of Norse and Teutonic sagas, or of Oriental epigrams, or of Italian love lyrics of the early Renaissance. Robinson's language from the beginning was prosy—not elegant or precious—and it offered the illusion of the colloquial. Invariably accompanying this quality in Robinson's verse was a concern for balance or proportion which saved his diction from the banality and awkwardness of offhand prose statement. We see his characteristic hand in the opening of the sonnet, "The Clerks":

> I did not think that I should find them there
> When I came back again; but there they stood,
> As in the days they dreamed of when young blood
> Was in their cheeks and women called them fair.

This is a long prosaic unit which flirts with dullness. It gains distinction and animation from the nice division between the "I" and "I's" movement, and "they" and their unchanged reality. It achieves further vitality by subtle shifts in emphasis and tone involving "there," "their" and "them," "they."

We see the same kind of distinction at the beginning of "Captain Craig":

> I doubt if ten men in all Tilbury Town
> Had ever shaken hands with Captain Craig,
> Or called him by his name, or looked at him
> So curiously, or so concernedly,
> As they had looked at ashes; . . . .

The prosaic quality is here again, though the verbal elements are somewhat more complex. What elevates this passage, as well, is its balance—the separation of the plain statement of doubt from the more fanciful elaboration. We contrast the quiet, detached manner of the first two lines with the perceptive increase of the poet's concern, which is suggested by the repetition of the "or" and confirmed by the startling introduction of "ashes."

Robinson is modern in other ways—in his obvious delight in cultivating the ironic. He shares with the modern poets who follow him, Pound, Eliot, and Auden, certain very general attitudes which sustain the ironic tone: a distrust of appearance in modern life; a sense of the inadequacy of the feeling man, rather than the thinking man; and an affection for the device of the antihero. Captain Craig is very nearly the first of a whole set of shabby, defective characters who have in the twentieth century criticized our institutions and disturbed our complacency.

We consider the ironic heritage of Pound and Eliot as being mainly French, a gift of the iconoclastic poets of the nineteenth century, Corbière and Laforgue, with a lesser contribution from the English metaphysical poets. This heritage does not touch Robinson, whose apprenticeship to French verse, served in the early 1890's, was limited to formal experimentation in ballades, villanelles, and rondeaux in the spirit of Austin Dobson and the late Victorian Romantics. Cowper, Crabbe, Wordsworth, Browning, and Kipling meant far more to Robinson than did the English metaphysical poets. Robinson has his roots in irony closer to home, deriving something, perhaps, from the functional ambiguities of Nathaniel Hawthorne, whom he read with complete admiration in the 1890's, and from his own constitutional unreadiness to accept transcendental definitions of man and the world, definitions which he found attractive and satisfying in many ways.

The form of much of Robinson's irony emerges with great clarity from "Captain Craig." There is, on one hand, a view of man founded on the somber realities of the human condition and, on the other, a consciousness of man's possibilities sustained by intense philosophical idealism. The division is the point of one of the Captain's fables, the stories which the ailing, penniless old man tells for the instruction of the group of young men who keep him alive. The tale, in its tone and in its verbal mannerisms, resembles a Browning soliloquy, but the moral, the judgment passed upon the behavior of the Captain's selfish, shallow heroine, is unmistakably Robinsonian:

> "She gives enough,
> You say; but what is giving like hers worth?
> What is a gift without the soul to guide it?
> 'Poor dears, and they have cancers?—Oh!' she says;

> And away she works at that new altar-cloth
> For the Reverend Hieronymus Mackintosh—
> Third person, Jerry. 'Jerry,' she says, 'can say
> Such lovely things, and make life seem so sweet!'
> Jerry can drink, also.—And there she goes,
> Like a whirlwind through an orchard in the springtime—
> Throwing herself away as if she thought
> The world and the whole planetary circus
> Were a flourish of apple blossoms. Look at her!"

There would be no irony here without the references to the possibilities for genuine service which exist for the deluded heroine, unrealized though these are. They are suggested at points in the rush and fury of the lady's activity—in "cancers," "soul," and "The world and the whole planetary circus." These provide a larger perspective for the viewing of the new altar-cloth and a basis for sympathy for the real Jerry, who is not "so sweet."

Irony reinforces a tendency in Robinson's diction which makes for freshness and for a sound which seems contemporary. This is Robinson's practice of yoking terms coming from widely separated contexts. There may be a marriage of the spiritual and the domestic, as in "the doorway of God's home" (I of "Two Sonnets") and "Love's handsel" (II of "Two Sonnets"). The poet may join opposites in meaning like "squeamish and emasculate crusade" ("Zola"), "glory of Greek shame" ("Villanelle of Change"), "incessant scream of commerce ringing clear" ("Amaryllis") and "trumpet crash of blood-sick victory" ("L'Envoi"). There are times when Robinson's bold combinations seem questionable—when, indeed, the pervasive force of God's love becomes the homely "love's elemental overglow" ("Sonnet"—"When we can all so excellently give"), but there is no denying the success in "Captain Craig" of the "tribute of recriminating groans" or of the description of the old man's clutching fingers as being "icy warm."

The concern for accuracy in presenting dramatic situations and psychological states is responsible for complexity in Robinson's vocabulary too. We feel this drift in his language in *Captain Craig and Other Poems*, particularly in the massing of compound words. The Captain describes himself as "Sage-errant, favored of the Mysteries/ And self-reputed humorist at large," and he admits to a career of "world-worshiping,/ Time-questioning, sun-fearing, and heart-yielding." Damaris, the widow of "The Book of Annandale," comes to look at her reluctance to accept a new love and to begin a new life as "grave-deluded, flesh-bewildered fear."

Robinson introduces a wholly different sort of richness into his diction through his frequent allusion to light and music. The effect which he achieves by this is not the greater precision which the attention to irony, or psychology, or drama has forced, it is closer now to the mystical. The references to light and music point to a level of meaning which exists beyond the particular image, which precedes even the existence of the poem. Light stands often in Robinson's verse for the perception of spiritual truth, as in, say, "a shaft of God's eternal day" in "Supremacy," and music, for the essential truth itself (the "lost, imperial music" of "Credo") or for the harmonious thought or the fruitful life made possible by the acceptance of truth. Some lines from "The World" illustrate Robinson's use of both patterns of figures and his habitual tendency to combine them:

> For some there is a music all day long
> Like flutes in Paradise, they are so glad;
> And there is hell's eternal under-song
> Of curses and the cries of men gone mad.
>
> Some say the Scheme with love stands luminous,
> Some say 'twere better back to chaos hurled;

There are no other controlling figures in the early verse which Robinson relies upon as heavily as he does the light and music images. "Captain Craig" introduces an interesting complexity with the notion of a "demon in the sunlight," of the snares and pitfalls which exist for the well-meaning and the right-thinking. This new dimension for Robinson's traditional figures seems entirely appropriate in a comic work which records the vagrant Captain's progress toward the absolute. The older Robinson will explore the use of other controlling devices, appearing in the early poetry only as effective images in isolated poems: the garden, as representative of the completed or fulfilled life (in "Avon's Harvest" and "Mortmain"); the house or castle, to suggest the form of a man's worldly achievement (in *Cavender's House, Matthias at the Door, Lancelot*); the sea, to indicate the indifferent flow of time (in *Tristram* and *The Glory of the Nightingales*).

Robinson's narrative technique has attracted deservedly much contemporary critical interest. Conrad Aiken has linked Robinson and Henry James in the matter of narrative method, and it is easy to see why, if we are willing to compare the fictional devices of a narrative poet with those of a novelist. The poet shares with the novelist an interest in "relations and contacts (between character and character) always extraordinarily *conscious*,"[1] to use Aiken's description of the similarity. Both have a concern for integrity of point of view in their characters, an awareness of what is demanded to make the point of view consistent and convincing, and a fondness, considered excessive by many readers, for the analysis of motives and psychological effects.

We have a restricted view of Robinson's narrative practice in *Selected Early Poems and Letters*, since this edition contains none of the works of Robinson's great narrative period, which began with the first Arthurian piece, *Merlin*, in 1917. It does have the poet's early serious efforts at story telling, poems which are often highly successful in their own right and which acquire even greater significance when we read subsequently the long narratives of Robinson's maturity. "Captain Craig," in presenting a study of spiritual exploration and conversion, anticipates in handling these themes *The Man Who Died Twice*, a narrative poem that won a Pulitzer prize. "The Book of Annandale," with

---

[1] Conrad Aiken, *Collected Criticism of Conrad Aiken from 1916 to the Present: A Reviewer's ABC,* intro. Rufus A. Blanshard (New York: Meridian Books Inc., 1958), p. 342.

its intense preoccupation with the responses of two people to the same catastrophe, foreshadows in its meticulous examination of emotions Robinson's lengthy domestic dramas, *Roman Bartholow, Cavender's House, Matthias at the Door,* and *Talifer.* All of the early narratives reveal fictional devices and narrative approaches which Robinson was to employ with profit later in his career.

The most ambitious poem of Robinson's first volume is "The Night Before," a long, loose monologue of a murderer who is doomed to die for destroying his wife's lover. It is typical of Robinson that we should have in the poem not only the consciousness of the condemned man but the suggestion of another mind, that of the father-confessor, Dominie. There is very little interaction, it is true, since Dominie says nothing, only listens sympathetically. We are impressed, nevertheless, by what Dominie represents; he stands for the morals and values of the ordinary world, while the murderer seems an exotic deviant, a victim caught and wrung by impulses which he cannot control. The whole point of the monologue is to reduce the sense of difference separating the good man from the bad and to demonstrate how it is possible for human degradation and tragedy to be consequences of a concern for decency. Indeed, we learn that

> Virtue
> May flower in hell, when its roots are twisted
> And wound with the roots of vice . . . .

Poe's "Tamerlane" is a study much like "The Night Before" in the use of the inspired monologue to give meaning to an extraordinary life, even an abhorrent one in normal human terms, but the end of Poe's creative effort is to sustain the difference which divides Tamerlane from his father-confessor, whom the conqueror treats with a casualness close to contempt.

What is peculiarly Robinsonian in "The Night Before" is the absorption with the psyche of a victim, a creature cut off by nature or by accident from the normal and regular movements of the world. What seems untypical of Robinson in the poem and annoying to the modern reader is the sketchy, melodramatic plot line and the repetitive allusion, by exclamation and despairing apostrophe, to the victim's moral dilemma. The morality of the work seems pretentious and noisy—not as the older Robinson would present it, understated and implicit.

There is no melodrama in "Captain Craig," though the basic situation of the poem invites it. The Captain, a derelict and a sponge, converts a group of cynical and worldly young men, one of whom is the narrator, to his own ideal position. The shift in the attitudes of the good fellows of The Chrysalis tavern is managed with skill and at a pace which permits the Captain's reminiscences, fables, letters, and philosophical commentaries to have a gradual and a cumulative effect. The Captain talks a good deal about the necessity for discovering the primitive self, employing abstract discourse and dramatic demonstrations, but the essential narrative problem is not obscured: that is the precarious relationship existing between the pauper and his sponsors. Our age admires Robinson's close attention to the complicated responses of the narrator and his companions, ranging from open hostility to love, even if it must put on, at times, a tolerant face to the Captain's wordy idealism and sun worship.

There is little of the eloquence of Captain Craig in "The Book of Annandale," which consists entirely of the analysis of psychological effects. We observe the reactions of a man and a woman to the same problem, the death of a well-loved marriage partner. What concerns us in this juxtaposition of two quite different psyches is the extent of obligation to the dead and the attraction of possibilities for the renewal of life. The condensation, here, is almost excessive since we are hard put at times to discover the facts which will make a coherent whole from the tangled relationships of Annandale and Damaris. The poem has intensity and truth as domestic drama, and it prepares us for later and more extended Robinson narratives, exploring at depth the problems of fidelity, freedom, and happiness in marriage.

"Isaac and Archibald" and "Aunt Imogen" are, perhaps, the most successful poems in Robinson's *Captain Craig* volume

—that is, most satisfying in terms of the poet's evident objectives. The poems are not so ambitious and so experimental as is "Captain Craig"; nor are they so intense and so elliptical as is "The Book of Annandale." They have their subtleties too in narrative method and in characterization, more than sufficient to enlist the sympathy of the modern reader. In "Isaac and Archibald" we have the fortunate device of the boy observer, who views the reunion of the old men, Isaac and Archibald, and records what he sees and hears, and what his active imagination adds—primarily a new dimension in the landscape in which the old men become heroes of classical Greece. The character of Aunt Imogen has a rewarding complexity, though not that, certainly, of Damaris. We are moved by Imogen's "feminine paradox," the fact

> that she
> Who had so little sunshine for herself
> Should have so much for others.

All of Robinson's narratives remind us, sometimes with abruptness, that we are modern observers able to examine, with the perception that science and art have given us, action which is highly conscious and seldom obvious. None does this more successfully, perhaps, than Robinson's adaptation—extension, to be more accurate—of the Alcestis story, "As a World Would Have It." Here Robinson's problem is not that of Euripides, who described the noble sacrifice of Alcestis, who accepted death to save her husband, King Admetus, from an early grave, and the miracle of her return to earth as a result of the intercession of Heracles. Robinson is concerned with the reaction to the return —in Alcestis and in Admetus—and he meditates upon what is required for the husband and the wife to recapture something close to their old feeling for each other and what must occur for them to resume a pattern of life which had been broken in so spectacular a manner.

There is much in *Selected Early Poems,* in the technique of Robinson's poetry and in his method of narration, to establish Robinson as a modern poet, possibly our first. This claim, an obvious one in many ways, has been obscured by other facts about the poet, and these we should know as well. There is, for example, Robinson's continuing affection for traditional forms, the blank verse of his many long narratives, the rhymed verse in tetrameter and trimeter, and the sonnet. It is an affection which calls to mind the great Victorian poets but no considerable modern American poet except Robert Frost. There is the movement in Robinson's work from the short lyric—intense, original, and symptomatic of the poet's acute awareness of an inadequate world—to the ambitious and long dramatic narratives, projected on a large scale with the assistance of analogy, symbol, and direct allusion. We recognize in this the yearning for the "big" work which haunted the imaginations of the major poets of the last century, Tennyson, Browning, William Morris, and Longfellow, differing vastly otherwise in talent and in intellectual interests. Tying Robinson also to the nineteenth century is the persistent influence in his poetry of a form of philosophical idealism. This was originally close to Emerson's transcendentalism, but by *King Jasper* (1935), Robinson's last extended narrative, his idealism had been reduced to a stubborn faith in the power of the human mind and spirit to survive, despite the catastrophe which seemed to follow inevitably man's blind pursuit of the material. Finally, there is Robinson's belief in the elevated position of art. He was a poet, and becoming proficient in his art was for him a full-time assignment. He did not wish to earn his living by jobs unrelated to his talents, and his refusal to yield on this point, at times in the face of starvation, suggests the traditional attitude of the English poet (and the American poet too, with less consistency) toward worldly employment.

What do we conclude? The poems of this volume speak for themselves. We sense the modern spirit in Robinson despite the fact that he retained intellectual convictions and ideals which seem characteristic of the nineteenth century. The poet whom Robinson most resembles in this respect is Yeats, who also carried into the new century an affection for the literary forms and an appreciation of the artistic aspirations of an earlier day.

II. THE UNIQUE TALENT OF E. A. ROBINSON

Far too little has been written of Robinson's early achievement as a poet, when we think of the critical attention given justifiably to Yeats's early verse, though the American had to confront standards and conventions in poetry far more sterile than those in Dublin, London, and Paris. Robinson's background was Gardiner, Maine; Cambridge, Massachusetts; and New York. It is Gardiner, perhaps, that contributed most to the making of the poet—more, certainly, than the two years at Harvard College, where he picked up a proficiency in French and encountered idealism in various forms, philosophical and artistic, and more than his move to New York, where he acquired intellectual companions and discovered excitement in the theater and the opera house. The odd fact about Robinson is that he began, in a sense, as a mature poet, almost immediately conscious of his artistic goals and aware of his own powers and weaknesses. Robinson's earliest work, *The Torrent and The Night Before* and *The Children of the Night*, had strength and originality. This phenomenon requires explanation—an explanation which must begin in the 1890's.

The ideal standards for verse which had dominated American poetry since 1870, in publishing houses and in magazines, continued to exert a restrictive influence upon writing into the 1890's. Edmund Clarence Stedman, who with Bayard Taylor, Richard Henry Stoddard, and Thomas Bailey Aldrich had formed earlier an influential little group devoted to the pure and the beautiful in poetry, was the most considerable force in American poetry. True, there was some restive stirring, more than at any time since the mighty throb of Whitman's voice was stilled—almost—by paralysis in 1873. There was new life in the epigrammatic and cynical sketches of Stephen Crane, in Santayana's thoughtful, unsentimental sonnets on the nature of art and the power of the human intellect, in Emily Dickinson's intimate and provocative verses, just published in 1890, four years after her death, and even in Richard Hovey's zestful lyrics. But the most effective general influence was still that of Stedman, who placed his stamp upon the decade of the nineties (and all previous ones in America, for that matter) in *An American Anthology* (1900).

Stedman's esthetic doctrine, stated best in *The Nature and Elements of Poetry* (1892), seemed, to the superficial eye, Emersonian. Like Emerson, Stedman exalted the position of the poet, insisting that the artist was in harmony with the soul of the universe, but he is unlike Emerson when he comes to the problem of defining the powers of the poet. Emerson held that the poet dealt with the facts of the world, the "facts amidst appearances," the facts which were spiritual in nature. Stedman, on the other hand, claimed that it was the "investigator" who achieved knowledge of the scientific facts and that the poet must content himself with "the *semblances* known to eye, ear, and touch." [2] What is recorded here is a shift in authority which marks the difference between Emerson's comprehensive "idealism" and Stedman's limited "ideality." A direct consequence of Stedman's retreat concerns the matter of taste in art. Stedman rejected the "supercilious attitude of our transcendentalists toward their beloved mistress Beauty" [3]; in short, he conceived taste as an activity divorced from the total perception of the artist, in the Emersonian sense, and he invited more shallow standards of the pretty and the ornamental. It is these that dominate the poetry of the nineties and encourage the numerous solemn tributes to great men, valued institutions, and outstanding public occasions; the nostalgic and sentimental reminiscences of an earlier and better day; the excursions into the melodramatic, often enlivened by exotic backgrounds and references to historical events; and the constant lament, inevitably in archaic diction, about the material and prosaic age.

Now Robinson returned to Emerson too, but with a differ-

[2] Edmund Clarence Stedman, *The Nature and Elements of Poetry* (Boston: Houghton Mifflin Company, 1892), p. 28.

[3] *Ibid.*, p. 47.

ence. He sought to become a genuine Emersonian idealist, and not to edit transcendental doctrines to the point of their rejection, as Stedman had done. For Robinson, comprehensive idealism was a relief from the hard facts of his own immediate world, and he recorded in letters to his friends (Harry Smith, Arthur Gledhill, and George Latham, especially) his struggle to achieve calm and spiritual equilibrium in the face of domestic tragedy in Gardiner.

The facts were bitter. Robinson saw the general decline in his family's material fortune; the physical disintegration of both of his brothers, Dean and Herman, whose careers had looked so promising; and the death of his mother from "black diphtheria." At the same time he was troubled by his own failure to find a vocation which would gain a living.

Robinson did not wish to deny reality, as the proponents of ideality had in ignoring contemporary industrial society; he tried to reconcile the unpleasant facts of existence with a conception of a spiritual meaning for the world. The reconciliation was slow and painful, as the letters reveal, occurring largely in the years following Robinson's return from Harvard in 1893. One Robinson critic has called this episode in the poet's emotional life his "conversion to idealism." [4] "Conversion" may be too strong a term. At any rate, in December of 1896, shortly after the death of his mother, Robinson wrote solemnly: ". . . I am very glad to be able to stand up and say that I am an idealist. Perhaps idealism is the philosophy of desperation but I do not think so. To me it is the only logical and satisfactory theory of life." [5]

Robinson was not a comfortable idealist, though he was a sincere one. We cannot deny the power of his allusion to the

[4] Edmund S. Fussell, *Edwin Arlington Robinson: The Literary Background of a Traditional Poet* (Berkeley: University of California Press, 1954), p. 156.

[5] Letter to Harry de Forest Smith, December 7, 1896, in *Untriangulated Stars: Letters of Edwin Arlington Robinson to Harry de Forest Smith, 1890-1905,* ed. Denham Sutcliffe (Cambridge, Mass.: Harvard University Press, 1947), p. 264.

"light" and to "the imperial music," though we are frequently
puzzled by the leap of the imagination or the act of faith which
makes it possible for the poet to affirm "the coming glory of the
Light."}Little probability for the leap exists in "Credo"—as little,
say, as there is for the total understanding promised "ye builders" in "Kosmos." Ultimately Emerson, Carlyle, and Mary Baker
Eddy—the teachers most relied upon for spiritual training—were
not to satisfy Robinson. His idealism would give way before the
compulsion to reproduce the real world with accuracy. What
remained in Robinson was compassion and sympathy, even for
those human creatures, like Aaron Stark and the old man in
"The Pity of the Leaves," who move in worlds untouched by
any compensating spiritual principle. Robinson retained, too, a
deep feeling of purpose in the universe, a meaning which rested
in or behind the often puzzling processes of life.

The peculiar form of Robinson's spiritual development contributed heavily to his uniqueness as a poet in the 1890's. We
find the reasons for it in Gardiner. It is Gardiner that saved
Robinson from traditional mediocrity, as Ireland saved young
Yeats, perhaps, from pre-Raphaelite excesses. Robinson wanted
to reassert Emerson's comprehensive idealism at a time when
art and poetry seemed radically divorced from the complexities
of modern life, and he stood apart from contemporary sonnet
makers, verse dramatists, and chanters of odes, a somber shade
from his New England past. When his own experience had led
him to qualify Emerson and finally to push beyond him, Robinson was sustained by a sympathy for all of the crotchety details
of life, and he traced with loving care the histories of human
beings hopelessly caught in traps of various kinds. Some of the
most impressive poems in *The Torrent* and *The Children of the
Night*, "Luke Havergal," "The Pity of the Leaves," and "The
Chorus of Old Men in 'Aegeus,'" to name a few, are uncom-
promising sketches of defective life, consistent and moving without benefit of the rhetoric of "The Night Before" or the hope of
relief or change that might come from a higher, better world.
The higher world does make its appearance in "Captain

Craig," but it is not Emersonian in conception and not touched by the Emerson magic. The Captain achieves spiritual perception after he has accepted all of the degrading details of his own physical state, and that perception does little to alter or to explain his pathetic condition. Other poems in the "Captain Craig" volume approach the spiritual absolutes similarly in a somewhat tentative manner. The love which the poet feels for Lorraine (in "The Growth of 'Lorraine'") does not save her from the fate worse than death; it does prompt the suicide which terminates a life thrown away. The understanding which breaks the silence separating the poet and a potential friend (in "The Corridor") comes too late to have any satisfying result. And the wife of Palissy (in "The Wife of Palissy"), even after the great artistic discovery (the secret of white enamel) which made all the toil and privation a proper sacrifice to genius, refuses to apologize for her doubts and misgivings. We recognize that Robinson has created in these poems his own curious world in which the human organism fulfills itself strictly according to the pattern of its own nature and in which spiritual attributes are powerless to disturb the inexorable process.

The E. A. Robinson of 1901 was a mature poet who had broken away completely from the intellectual standards of his contemporaries. It was small wonder that Captain Craig had to travel so far and search so hard for a publisher. Three publishing houses rejected him, and Robinson could say with accuracy and with brave confidence: "His trousers are pretty badly frayed, and his general appearance seems to be more and more disreputable on each return; but perhaps that is all right. He is a sort of disreputable cuss, anyhow . . . ." [6] One house did accept him finally, but only after a financial subsidy had come from friends in Gardiner. If Gardiner must bear, then, a major responsibility for Robinson's uniqueness, Gardiner it was, too, that made his difference a matter of public record and forced his recognition as a great artist, perhaps the first great poet of the new century.

[6] Letter to Daniel Gregory Mason, September 20, 1901, in *Selected Letters of Edwin Arlington Robinson,* ed. Ridgely Torrence (New York: The Macmillan Company, 1940), p. 45.

1869	Edwin Arlington Robinson born at Head Tide, Maine, on December 22, the third son of Edward and Mary Robinson.
1870	Family moved to Gardiner, Maine.
1888	Graduated from Gardiner High School.
1889	Completed a year of post-graduate study (in Horace and Milton) at Gardiner High School.
1890	A sonnet "Thalia" and a blank verse translation of the galley race in Book V of the *Aeneid* published in the *Reporter Monthly* (Gardiner, Me.).
1891-1893	Attended Harvard College as a "special student"; published in *The Harvard Advocate,* but not in *The Harvard Monthly.*
1892	Edward Robinson died.
1893	Returned to Gardiner. Robinson family suffered heavy financial loss in the collapse of Western real estate.
1893-1895	Attempted without success to write fiction that would sell.
1894-1896	Engaged intermittently, with a friend Harry de Forest Smith, a classicist, in making a metrical translation of Sophocles' *Antigone.*
1896	*The Torrent and The Night Before,* published at his own expense and printed by the Riverside Press, Cambridge, Mass. Mary Robinson died in November of "black diphtheria."
1897	*The Children of the Night,* published by Richard Badger and Company, Boston, Mass. Moved to New York at the end of the year.

1898   Returned to Gardiner in May because of a lack of money.

1899   Employed as President Eliot's confidential clerk at Harvard College from January to June.

Returned to New York in October.

1902   *Captain Craig*, finally published by Houghton, Mifflin and Company, Boston and New York, after the manuscript of the poems had been rejected by Scribner's (New York) and lost by Small, Maynard and Company (Boston).

1903-1904   Worked as a time-checker in the construction of the first New York subway.

1905   Appointed in June by President Theodore Roosevelt, an admirer of *The Children of the Night*, to a post in the New York Custom House. *The Children of the Night* reprinted by Scribner's in October as a consequence of the President's interest, which is recorded in a critical article in *The Outlook* (August 12).

1906-1909   Unsuccessful efforts to write prose plays for Broadway production; completed *Ferguson's Ivory Tower* (later entitled *Van Zorn*) and *The Porcupine*.

1909   Left New York Custom House.

1910   *The Town Down the River* (Scribner's).

1910-1913   Attempted again without success to write prose fiction and drama.

1911   Spent his first summer at The MacDowell Colony, Peterborough, New Hampshire, to which he returned regularly in subsequent summers.

1914   The Macmillan Company (New York) became Robinson's publisher, when Scribner's refused to publish his plays.

Van Zorn.

1915   *The Porcupine. Captain Craig* revised and reprinted.

1916   *The Man Against the Sky.*

1917   Received on January 1 a gift of money from anonymous donors, a gift which was administered by the New York Trust Company and renewed regularly until 1922, when he no longer needed it.

Merlin.

1920   *Lancelot,* by Thomas Seltzer Inc. (New York), when Macmillan, because of the poor sale of *Merlin,* refused to risk publication.

The Three Taverns.

1921   *Avon's Harvest.*
         Collected Poems.
         Pulitzer prize for poetry.

1922   British edition of *Collected Poems,* with an introduction by John Drinkwater.
         Doctor of Letters from Yale University.

1923   *Roman Bartholow.*
         Sailed for England, April 18; departed from England, July 26.

1924   *The Man Who Died Twice.*
         Second Pulitzer prize for poetry.

1925   *Dionysus in Doubt.*
         Doctor of Letters from Bowdoin College.

1927   *Tristram.*
         Third Pulitzer prize for poetry.

1928   *Sonnets: 1889-1927.*

1929   "Introduction" to the *Letters of Thomas Sergeant Perry.*
         Cavender's House.

1930   *The Glory of the Nightingales.*

1931   *Selected Poems,* with a preface by Bliss Perry.
         Matthias at the Door.

1932   *Nicodemus.*

1933   *Talifer.*

1934   *Amaranth.*

1935   Died in New York Hospital on April 6.
         King Jasper.

❧ ❧ ❧

SELECTED BIBLIOGRAPHY

BIBLIOGRAPHIES

HOGAN, CHARLES B., *A Bibliography of the Writings of Edwin Arlington Robinson*. New Haven: Yale University Press, 1936.

LIPPINCOTT, LILLIAN, *A Bibliography of the Writings and Criticisms of Edwin Arlington Robinson*. Boston: The F. W. Faxon Company, 1937.

Literary History of the United States, ed. R. E. Spiller, Willard Thorp, T. H. Johnson, H. S. Canby. New York: The Macmillan Company, 1948, III, 705-708.

Bibliography Supplement, Literary History of the United States, ed. Richard M. Ludwig. New York: The Macmillan Company, 1959, pp. 184-185.

LEARY, LEWIS, *Articles on American Literature, 1900-1950.* Durham, N.C.: Duke University Press, 1954, pp. 258-263.

WORKS

The Torrent and The Night Before. Printed for the author by The Riverside Press, Cambridge, Mass., 1896.

The Children of the Night: A Book of Poems. Boston: Richard G. Badger and Company, 1897.

Captain Craig: A Book of Poems. Boston and New York: Houghton, Mifflin and Company, 1902.

The Town Down the River: A Book of Poems. New York: Charles Scribner's Sons, 1910.

Van Zorn: A Comedy in Three Acts. New York: The Macmillan Company, 1914.

The Porcupine: A Drama in Three Acts. New York: The Macmillan Company, 1915.

The Man Against the Sky: A Book of Poems. New York: The Macmillan Company, 1916.

Merlin: A Poem. New York: The Macmillan Company, 1917.

Lancelot: A Poem. New York: Thomas Seltzer, 1920.

The Three Taverns: A Book of Poems. New York: The Macmillan Company, 1920.

Avon's Harvest. New York: The Macmillan Company, 1921.

Collected Poems. New York: The Macmillan Company, 1921.

Roman Bartholow. New York: The Macmillan Company, 1923.

The Man Who Died Twice. New York: The Macmillan Company, 1924.

Dionysus in Doubt: A Book of Poems. New York: The Macmillan Company, 1925.

Tristram. New York: The Macmillan Company, 1927.

Collected Poems. New York: The Macmillan Company, 1927, 5 vols.

Three Poems. Pirated edition printed in Cambridge, Mass., 1928.

Fortunatus. Reno: The Slide Mountain Press, 1928.

Sonnets: 1889-1927. New York: The Macmillan Company, 1928.

Modred: A Fragment. New York, New Haven, Princeton: The Brick Row Bookshop, Inc., 1929.

Cavender's House. New York: The Macmillan Company, 1929.

The Prodigal Son. New York: Random House, 1929.

Collected Poems. New York: The Macmillan Company, 1929.

Selections from the Letters of Thomas Sergeant Perry. An Edition with an Introduction. New York: The Macmillan Company, 1929.

The Valley of the Shadow. San Francisco: Yerba Buena Press, 1930.

The Glory of the Nightingales. New York: The Macmillan Company, 1930.

Selected Poems, with a Preface by Bliss Perry. New York: The Macmillan Company, 1931.

Matthias at the Door. New York: The Macmillan Company, 1931.

Nicodemus: A Book of Poems. New York: The Macmillan Company, 1932.

Talifer. New York: The Macmillan Company, 1933.

Amaranth. New York: The Macmillan Company, 1934.

King Jasper. Introduction by Robert Frost. New York: The Macmillan Company, 1935.

Hannibal Brown, Posthumous Poem. Buffalo, N.Y.: M. Klinke, 1936.

Collected Poems. New York: The Macmillan Company, 1937.

Tilbury Town: Selected Poems of Edwin Arlington Robinson. Introduction and Notes by Lawrance Thompson. New York: The Macmillan Company, 1953.

LETTERS

Selected Letters of Edwin Arlington Robinson. Introduction by Ridgely Torrence. New York: The Macmillan Company, 1940.

Untriangulated Stars: Letters of Edwin Arlington Robinson to Harry de Forest Smith, 1890-1905. Edited by Denham Sutcliffe. Cambridge, Mass.: Harvard University Press, 1947.

BIOGRAPHICAL AND CRITICAL STUDIES

AIKEN, CONRAD, *Collected Criticism of Conrad Aiken from 1916 to the Present: A Reviewer's ABC* (In the essays on Robinson). New York: Meridian Books, 1958.

BARNARD, ELLSWORTH, *Edwin Arlington Robinson: A Critical Study.* New York: The Macmillan Company, 1952.

CESTRE, CHARLES, *An Introduction to Edwin Arlington Robinson.* New York: The Macmillan Company, 1930.

FUSSELL, EDWIN SILL, *Edwin Arlington Robinson, The Literary Background of a Traditional Poet.* Berkeley: University of California Press, 1954.

GREGORY, HORACE, and MARYA ZATURENSKA, *A History of American Poetry (1900-1940).* New York: Harcourt, Brace and Company, 1946, pp. 107-132.

HAGEDORN, HERMANN, *Edwin Arlington Robinson: A Biography*. New York: The Macmillan Company, 1938.

KAPLAN, ESTELLE, *Philosophy in the Poetry of Edwin Arlington Robinson*. New York: Columbia University Press, 1940.

LOWELL, AMY, *Tendencies in Modern American Poetry*. New York: The Macmillan Company, 1917, pp. 3-75.

MORRIS, LLOYD R., *The Poetry of Edwin Arlington Robinson*. New York: George H. Doran Company, 1923.

NEFF, EMERY E., *Edwin Arlington Robinson*. New York: William Sloane Associates, 1948.

REDMAN, BEN RAY, *Edwin Arlington Robinson*. New York: Robert M. McBride and Company, 1926.

RICHARDS, LAURA E., *E.A.R.* Cambridge, Mass.: Harvard University Press, 1936.

VAN DOREN, MARK, *Edwin Arlington Robinson*. New York: The Literary Guild of America, 1927.

WINTERS, YVOR, *Edwin Arlington Robinson*. Norfolk, Conn.: New Directions Books, 1946.

One article that is especially illuminating about "Captain Craig" is W. Denham Sutcliffe's "The Original of Robinson's Captain Craig," *The New England Quarterly*, XVI (September, 1943), 409-415.

❀ ❀ ❀

TEXTUAL NOTE

The text for Robinson's poems comes from *The Torrent and The Night Before* (Printed for the author by The Riverside Press, Cambridge, Mass., 1896), *The Children of the Night: A Book of Poems* (Boston: R. C. Badger and Company, 1897), and *Captain Craig: A Book of Poems* (Boston and New York: Houghton, Mifflin and Company, 1902). I have accepted as definitive for *Selected Early Poems and Letters* the text in *The Children of the Night* for the poems published earlier in *The Torrent and The Night Before* and reprinted in *The Children of the Night*. The editions of Robinson's *Collected Poems,* beginning with that of 1921 (New York: The Macmillan Company), show continued textual revision of some of the poems found here—especially of "Captain Craig," "Isaac and Archibald," and "Aunt Imogen."

I have taken the letters to Harry de Forest Smith from Denham Sutcliffe's *Untriangulated Stars: Letters of Edwin Arlington Robinson to Harry de Forest Smith, 1890-1905* (Cambridge, Mass.: Harvard University Press, 1947), and those to Daniel Gregory Mason and Josephine Preston Peabody from *Selected Letters of Edwin Arlington Robinson* (New York: The Macmillan Company, 1940), edited by Robinson's friend, the poet Ridgely Torrence. I wish to acknowledge my indebtedness to the Harvard University Press and the Harvard University Library for permission to reprint Robinson's letters, and I wish to thank the librarians of Houghton Library and Harvard University for allowing me to examine the originals of many of the letters which I have reprinted here.

Finally I must thank my colleague, Professor Lawrance Thompson; Miss Grace Briggs of the Harvard University Press; Mrs. Cornelia Lively of Princeton; and my wife, Jeanne C. Davis, for various contributions to the accuracy of the text of *Selected Early Poems and Letters.*

Early Poems

Early Poems

THE TORRENT

I found a torrent falling in a glen
Where the sun's light shone silvered and leaf-split;
The boom, the foam, and the mad flash of it
All made a magic symphony; but when
I thought upon the coming of hard men   5
To cut those patriarchal trees away,
And turn to gold the silver of that spray,
I shuddered. Yet a gladness now and then
Did wake me to myself till I was glad
In earnest, and was welcoming the time   10
For screaming saws to sound above the chime
Of idle waters, and for me to know
The jealous visionings that I had had
Were steps to the great place where trees and torrents go.

AARON STARK

Withal a meagre man was Aaron Stark,—
Cursed and unkempt, shrewd, shrivelled, and morose.
A miser was he, with a miser's nose,
And eyes like little dollars in the dark.
His thin, pinched mouth was nothing but a mark;   5
And when he spoke there came like sullen blows
Through scattered fangs a few snarled words and close,
As if a cur were chary of its bark.

Glad for the murmur of his hard renown,
Year after year he shambled through the town,— 10
A loveless exile moving with a staff;
And oftentimes there crept into his ears
A sound of alien pity, touched with tears,—
And then (and only then) did Aaron laugh.

THE DEAD VILLAGE

Here there is death. But even here, they say,—
Here where the dull sun shines this afternoon
As desolate as ever the dead moon
Did glimmer on dead Sardis,—men were gay;
And there were little children here to play, 5
With small soft hands that once did keep in tune
The strings that stretch from heaven, till too soon
The change came, and the music passed away.

Now there is nothing but the ghosts of things,—
No life, no love, no children, and no men; 10
And over the forgotten place there clings
The strange and unrememberable light
That is in dreams. The music failed, and then
God frowned, and shut the village from His sight.

BALLADE OF A SHIP

Down by the flash of the restless water
  The dim White Ship like a white bird lay;
Laughing at life and the world they sought her,
  And out she swung to the silvering bay.
  Then off they flew on their roystering way, 5
And the keen moon fired the light foam flying
  Up from the flood where the faint stars play,
And the bones of the brave in the wave are lying.

'Twas a king's fair son with a king's fair daughter,
  And full three hundred beside, they say,—   10
Revelling on for the lone, cold slaughter
  So soon to seize them and hide them for aye;
  But they danced and they drank and their souls grew gay,
  Nor ever they knew of a ghoul's eye spying
  Their splendor a flickering phantom to stray   15
Where the bones of the brave in the wave are lying.

Through the mist of a drunken dream they brought her
  (This wild white bird) for the sea-fiend's prey:
The pitiless reef in his hard clutch caught her,
  And hurled her down where the dead men stay.   20
  A torturing silence of wan dismay—
Shrieks and curses of mad souls dying—
  Then down they sank to slumber and sway
Where the bones of the brave in the wave are lying.

ENVOY

Prince, do you sleep to the sound alway   25
  Of the mournful surge and the sea-birds' crying?—
Or does love still shudder and steel still slay,
  Where the bones of the brave in the wave are lying?

DEAR FRIENDS

Dear friends, reproach me not for what I do,
Nor counsel me, nor pity me; nor say
That I am wearing half my life away
For bubble-work that only fools pursue.
And if my bubbles be too small for you,   5
Blow bigger then your own: the games we play
To fill the frittered minutes of a day,
Good glasses are to read the spirit through.

And whoso reads may get him some shrewd skill;
And some unprofitable scorn resign,   10
To praise the very thing that he deplores;
So, friends (dear friends), remember, if you will,
The shame I win for singing is all mine,
The gold I miss for dreaming is all yours.

SONNET

When we can all so excellently give
The measure of love's wisdom with a blow,—
Why can we not in turn receive it so,
And end this murmur for the life we live?
And when we do so frantically strive   5
To win strange faith, why do we shun to know
That in love's elemental over-glow
God's wholeness gleams with light superlative?

Oh, brother men, if you have eyes at all,
Look at a branch, a bird, a child, a rose,—   10
Or anything God ever made that grows,—
Nor let the smallest vision of it slip,
Till you can read, as on Belshazzar's wall,
The glory of eternal partnership!

HER EYES

Up from the street and the crowds that went,
    Morning and midnight, to and fro,
Still was the room where his days he spent,
    And the stars were bleak, and the nights were slow.

Year after year, with his dream shut fast,   5
   He suffered and strove till his eyes were dim,
For the love that his brushes had earned at last,—
   And the whole world rang with the praise of him.

But he cloaked his triumph, and searched, instead,
   Till his cheeks were sere and his hairs were gray.   10
"There are women enough, God knows," he said. . . .
   "There are stars enough—when the sun's away."

Then he went back to the same still room
   That had held his dream in the long ago,
When he buried his days in a nameless tomb,   15
   And the stars were bleak, and the nights were slow.

And a passionate humor seized him there—
   Seized him and held him until there grew
Like life on his canvas, glowing and fair,
   A perilous face—and an angel's, too.   20

Angel and maiden, and all in one,—
   All but the eyes.—They were there, but yet
They seemed somehow like a soul half done.
   What was the matter? Did God forget? . . .

But he wrought them at last with a skill so sure   25
   That her eyes were the eyes of a deathless woman,—
With a gleam of heaven to make them pure,
   And a glimmer of hell to make them human.

God never forgets.—And he worships her
   There in that same still room of his,   30
For his wife, and his constant arbiter
   Of the world that was and the world that is.

And he wonders yet what her love could be
    To punish him after that strife so grim;
But the longer he lives with her eyes to see,   35
    The plainer it all comes back to him.

SONNET

    The master and the slave go hand in hand,
    Though touch be lost. The poet is a slave,
    And there be kings do sorrowfully crave
    The joyance that a scullion may command.
    But, ah, the sonnet-slave must understand   5
    The mission of his bondage, or the grave
    May clasp his bones, or ever he shall save
    The perfect word that is the poet's wand!

    The sonnet is a crown, whereof the rhymes
    Are for Thought's purest gold the jewel-stones;   10
    But shapes and echoes that are never done
    Will haunt the workshop, as regret sometimes
    Will bring with human yearning to sad thrones
    The crash of battles that are never won.

ZOLA

Because he puts the compromising chart
Of hell before your eyes, you are afraid;
Because he counts the price that you have paid
For innocence, and counts it from the start,
You loathe him. But he sees the human heart   5
Of God meanwhile, and in God's hand has weighed
Your squeamish and emasculate crusade
Against the grim dominion of his art.

Never until we conquer the uncouth
Connivings of our shamed indifference   10
(We call it Christian faith!) are we to scan
The racked and shrieking hideousness of Truth
To find, in hate's polluted self-defence
Throbbing, the pulse, the divine heart of man.

BALLADE OF BROKEN FLUTES

(*To A. T. Schumann*)

In dreams I crossed a barren land,
  A land of ruin, far away;
Around me hung on every hand
  A deathful stillness of decay;
  And silent, as in bleak dismay   5
That song should thus forsaken be,
  On that forgotten ground there lay
The broken flutes of Arcady.

The forest that was all so grand
  When pipes and tabors had their sway   10
Stood leafless now, a ghostly band
  Of skeletons in cold array.
  A lonely surge of ancient spray
Told of an unforgetful sea,
  But iron blows had hushed for aye   15
The broken flutes of Arcady.

No more by summer breezes fanned,
  The place was desolate and gray;
But still my dream was to command

New life into that shrunken clay.   20
I tried it. Yes, you scan to-day,
With uncommiserating glee,
    The songs of one who strove to play
The broken flutes of Arcady.

ENVOY

So, Rock, I join the common fray,   25
    To fight where Mammon may decree;
And leave, to crumble as they may,
    The broken flutes of Arcady.

FOR SOME POEMS BY MATTHEW ARNOLD

Sweeping the chords of Hellas with firm hand,
He wakes lost echoes from song's classic shore,
And brings their crystal cadence back once more
To touch the clouds and sorrows of a land
Where God's truth, cramped and fettered with a band   5
Of iron creeds, he cheers with golden lore
Of heroes and the men that long before
Wrought the romance of ages yet unscanned.

Still does a cry through sad Valhalla go
For Balder, pierced with Lok's unhappy spray—   10
For Balder, all but spared by Frea's charms;
And still does art's imperial vista show,
On the hushed sands of Oxus, far away,
Young Sohrab dying in his father's arms.

GEORGE CRABBE

Give him the darkest inch your shelf allows,
Hide him in lonely garrets, if you will,—
But his hard, human pulse is throbbing still
With the sure strength that fearless truth endows.
In spite of all fine science disavows,   5
Of his plain excellence and stubborn skill
There yet remains what fashion cannot kill,
Though years have thinned the laurel from his brows.

Whether or not we read him, we can feel
From time to time the vigor of his name   10
Against us like a finger for the shame
And emptiness of what our souls reveal
In books that are as altars where we kneel
To consecrate the flicker, not the flame.

SONNET

Oh for a poet—for a beacon bright
To rift this changless glimmer of dead gray;
To spirit back the Muses, long astray,
And flush Parnassus with a newer light;
To put these little sonnet-men to flight   5
Who fashion, in a shrewd, mechanic way,
Songs without souls, that flicker for a day,
To vanish in irrevocable night.

What does it mean, this barren age of ours?
Here are the men, the women, and the flowers,   10

The seasons, and the sunset, as before.
What does it mean? Shall not one bard arise
To wrench one banner from the western skies,
And mark it with his name forevermore?

THE ALTAR

Alone, remote, nor witting where I went,
I found an altar builded in a dream—
A fiery place, whereof there was a gleam
So swift, so searching, and so eloquent
Of upward promise, that love's murmur, blent   5
With sorrow's warning, gave but a supreme
Unending impulse to that human stream
Whose flood was all for the flame's fury bent.

Alas! I said,—the world is in the wrong.
But the same quenchless fever of unrest   10
That thrilled the foremost of that martyred throng
Thrilled me, and I awoke . . . and was the same
Bewildered insect plunging for the flame
That burns, and must burn somehow for the best.

THE HOUSE ON THE HILL

They are all gone away,
    The House is shut and still,
There is nothing more to say.

Through broken walls and gray
    The winds blow bleak and shrill: 5
They are all gone away.

Nor is there one to-day
  To speak them good or ill:
There is nothing more to say.

Why is it then we stray   10
  Around that sunken sill?
They are all gone away,

And our poor fancy-play
  For them is wasted skill:
There is nothing more to say.   15

There is ruin and decay
  In the House on the Hill:
They are all gone away,
There is nothing more to say.

THE WILDERNESS

Come away! come away! there's a frost along the marshes,
And a frozen wind that skims the shoal where it shakes the dead
  black water;
There's a moan across the lowland and a wailing through the
  woodland
Of a dirge that sings to send us back to the arms of those that
  love us.
There is nothing left but ashes now where the crimson chills of
  autumn   5
Put off the summer's languor with a touch that made us glad
For the glory that is gone from us, with a flight we cannot fol-
  low,
To the slopes of other valleys and the sounds of other shores.

Come away! come away! you can hear them calling, calling,
Calling us to come to them, and roam no more.   10
Over there beyond the ridges and the land that lies between us,
There's an old song calling us to come!

Come away! come away!—for the scenes we leave behind us
Are barren for the lights of home and a flame that's young for-
    ever;
And the lonely trees around us creak the warning of the night-
    wind,   15
That love and all the dreams of love are away beyond the moun-
    tains.
The songs that call for us to-night, they have called for men
    before us,
And the winds that blow the message, they have blown ten
    thousand years;
But this will end our wander-time, for we know the joy that
    waits us
In the strangeness of home-coming, and a faithful woman's
    eyes.   20

Come away! come away! there is nothing now to cheer us—
Nothing now to comfort us, but love's road home:—
Over there beyond the darkness there's a window gleams to greet
    us,
And a warm hearth waits for us within.

Come away! come away!—or the roving-fiend will hold us,   25
And make us all to dwell with him to the end of human faring:
There are no men yet can leave him when his hands are clutched
    upon them,
There are none will own his enmity, there are none will call him
    brother.
So we'll be up and on the way, and the less we brag the better
For the freedom that God gave us and the dread we do not
    know:—   30

The frost that skips the willow-leaf will again be back to blight
    it,
And the doom we cannot fly from is the doom we do not see.

Come away! come away! there are dead men all around us—
Frozen men that mock us with a wild, hard laugh
That shrieks and sinks and whimpers in the shrill November
    rushes,   35
And the long fall wind on the lake.

LUKE HAVERGAL

Go to the western gate, Luke Havergal,—   3
There where the vines cling crimson on the wall,—
And in the twilight wait for what will come.
The wind will moan, the leaves will whisper some—
Whisper of her, and strike you as they fall;   5
But go, and if you trust her she will call.
Go to the western gate, Luke Havergal—
Luke Havergal.

No, there is not a dawn in eastern skies
To rift the fiery night that's in your eyes;   10
But there, where western glooms are gathering,
The dark will end the dark, if anything:
God slays Himself with every leaf that flies,
And hell is more than half of paradise.
No, there is not a dawn in eastern skies—
In eastern skies.

Out of a grave I come to tell you this,—
Out of a grave I come to quench the kiss
That flames upon your forehead with a glow

That blinds you to the way that you must go.   20
Yes, there is yet one way to where she is,—
Bitter, but one that faith can never miss.
Out of a grave I come to tell you this—
To tell you this.

There is the western gate, Luke Havergal,   25
There are the crimson leaves upon the wall.
Go,—for the winds are tearing them away,—
Nor think to riddle the dead words they say,
Nor any more to feel them as they fall;
But go! and if you trust her she will call.   30
There is the western gate, Luke Havergal—
Luke Havergal.

THE CHORUS OF OLD MEN IN "ÆGEUS"

Ye gods that have a home beyond the world,
Ye that have eyes for all man's agony,
Ye that have seen this woe that we have seen,—
Look with a just regard,
And with an even grace,   5
Here on the shattered corpse of a shattered king,
Here on a suffering world where men grow old
And wander like sad shadows till, at last,
Out of the flare of life,
Out of the whirl of years,   10
Into the mist they go,
Into the mist of death.

O shades of you that loved him long before
The cruel threads of that black sail were spun,
May loyal arms and ancient welcomings   15

Receive him once again
Who now no longer moves
Here in this flickering dance of changing days,
Where a battle is lost and won for a withered wreath,
And the black master Death is over all,   20
To chill with his approach,
To level with his touch,
The reigning strength of youth,
The fluttered heart of age.

Woe for the fateful day when Delphi's word was lost—   25
Woe for the loveless prince of Æthra's line!
Woe for a father's tears and the curse of a king's release—
Woe for the wings of pride and the shafts of doom!—
And thou, the saddest wind
That ever blew from Crete,   30
Sing the fell tidings back to that thrice unhappy ship!—
Sing to the western flame,
Sing to the dying foam,
A dirge for the sundered years and a dirge for the years to be!

Better his end had been as the end of a cloudless day,   35
Bright, by the word of Zeus, with a golden star,
Wrought of a golden fame, and flung to the central sky,
To gleam on a stormless tomb for evermore:—
Whether or not there fell
To the touch of an alien hand   40
The sheen of his purple robe and the shine of his diadem,
Better his end had been
To die as an old man dies,—
But the fates are ever the fates, and a crown is ever a crown.

THE MIRACLE

"Dear brother, dearest friend, when I am dead,
And you shall see no more this face of mine,
Let nothing but red roses be the sign
Of the white life I lost for him," she said;
"No, do not curse him,—pity him instead;   5
Forgive him!—forgive me! . . God's anodyne
For human hate is pity; and the wine
That makes men wise, forgiveness. I have read
Love's message in love's murder, and I die."
And so they laid her just where she would lie,—   10
Under red roses. Red they bloomed and fell;
But when flushed autumn and the snows went by,
And spring came,—lo, from every bud's green shell
Burst a white blossom.—Can love reason why?

HORACE TO LEUCONOË

I pray you not, Leuconoë, to pore
With unpermitted eyes on what may be
Appointed by the gods for you and me,
Nor on Chaldean figures any more.
'T were infinitely better to implore   5
The present only:—whether Jove decree
More winters yet to come, or whether he
Make even this, whose hard, wave-eaten shore
Shatters the Tuscan seas to-day, the last—
Be wise withal, and rack your wine, nor fill   10

Your bosom with large hopes; for while I sing,
The envious close of time is narrowing;—
So seize the day,—or ever it be past,—
And let the morrow come for what it will.

BALLADE OF DEAD FRIENDS

As we the withered ferns
  By the roadway lying,
Time, the jester, spurns
  All our prayers and prying—
  All our tears and sighing,   5
Sorrow, change, and woe—
  All our where-and-whying
For friends that come and go.

Life awakes and burns,
  Age and death defying,   10
Till at last it learns
  All but Love is dying;
  Love's the trade we're plying,
God has willed it so;
  Shrouds are what we're buying   15
For friends that come and go.

Man forever yearns
  For the thing that's flying.
Everywhere he turns,
  Men to dust are drying,—   20
  Dust that wanders, eying
(With eyes that hardly glow)
  New faces, dimly spying
For friends that come and go.

ENVOY

And thus we all are nighing   25
    The truth we fear to know:
Death will end our crying
    For friends that come and go.

VILLANELLE OF CHANGE

Since Persia fell at Marathon,
    The yellow years have gathered fast:
Long centuries have come and gone.

And yet (they say) the place will don
    A phantom fury of the past,   5
Since Persia fell at Marathon;

And as of old, when Helicon
    Trembled and swayed with rapture vast
(Long centuries have come and gone),

This ancient plain, when night comes on,   10
    Shakes to a ghostly battle-blast,
Since Persia fell at Marathon.

But into soundless Acheron
    The glory of Greek shame was cast:
Long centuries have come and gone,   15

The suns of Hellas have all shone,
    The first has fallen to the last:—
Since Persia fell at Marathon,
Long centuries have come and gone.

THOMAS HOOD

The man who cloaked his bitterness within
This winding-sheet of puns and pleasantries,
God never gave to look with common eyes
Upon a world of anguish and of sin:
His brother was the branded man of Lynn;   5
And there are woven with his jollities
The nameless and eternal tragedies
That render hope and hopelessness akin.

We laugh, and crown him; but anon we feel
A still chord sorrow-swept,—a weird unrest;   10
And thin dim shadows home to midnight steal,
As if the very ghost of mirth were dead—
As if the joys of time to dreams had fled,
Or sailed away with Ines to the West.

FOR A BOOK BY THOMAS HARDY

With searching feet, through dark circuitous ways,
I plunged and stumbled; round me, far and near,
Quaint hordes of eyeless phantoms did appear,
Twisting and turning in a bootless chase,—
When, like an exile given by God's grace   5
To feel once more a human atmosphere,
I caught the world's first murmur, large and clear,
Flung from a singing river's endless race.

Then, through a magic twilight from below,
I heard its grand sad song as in a dream: 10

Life's wild infinity of mirth and woe
It sang me; and, with many a changing gleam,
Across the music of its onward flow
I saw the cottage lights of Wessex beam.

SUPREMACY

There is a drear and lonely tract of hell
From all the common gloom removed afar:
A flat, sad land it is, where shadows are,
Whose lorn estate my verse may never tell.
I walked among them and I knew them well: 5
Men I had slandered on life's little star
For churls and sluggards; and I knew the scar
Upon their brows of woe ineffable.

But as I went majestic on my way,
Into the dark they vanished, one by one,   10
Till, with a shaft of God's eternal day,
The dream of all my glory was undone,—
And, with a fool's importunate dismay,
I heard the dead men singing in the sun.

THREE QUATRAINS

I

As long as Fame's imperious music rings
    Will poets mock it with crowned words august;
And haggard men will clamber to be kings
    As long as Glory weighs itself in dust.

II

Drink to the splendor of the unfulfilled,   5
  Nor shudder for the revels that are done:
The wines that flushed Lucullus are all spilled,
  The strings that Nero fingered are all gone.

III

We cannot crown ourselves with everything,
  Nor can we coax the Fates for us to quarrel: 10
No matter what we are, or what we sing,
  Time finds a withered leaf in every laurel.

FOR CALDERON

And now, my brother, it is time   4
For me to tell the truth to you:
To tell the story of a crime
As black as Mona's eyes were blue.—
Yes, here to-night, before I die,   5
I'll speak the words that burn in me;
And you may send them, bye-and-bye,
To Calderon across the sea.

Now get some paper and a pen,
And sit right here, beside my bed.   10
Write every word I say, and then—
And then . . . well, what then?—I'll be dead!—
. . . But here I am alive enough
And I remember all I've done . . .
God knows what I was thinking of!—   15
But send it home—to Calderon.

And you, Francisco, brother, say,—
What is there for a man like me?—
I tell you God sounds far away—
As far—almost as far—as she!   20
I killed her! . . . Yes, I poisoned her—
So slowly that she never knew . . .
Francisco,—I'm a murderer.—
Now tell me what there is to do!

To die—of course; but after that,   25
I wonder if I live again!
And if I live again, for what?—
To suffer? . . . Bah!—there is no pain
But one; and that I know so well
That I can shame the devil's eyes! . . .   30
For twenty years I've heard in hell
What Mona sings in Paradise!

Strange, that a little Northern girl
Should love my brother Calderon,
And set my brain so in a whirl   35
That I was mad till she was gone! . . .
I wonder if all men be such
As I?—I wonder what love is!—
I never loved her very much
Until I saw she was his;—   40

And then I knew that I was lost:
And then—I knew that I was mad.—
I reasoned what it all would cost,
But that was nothing.—I was glad
To feel myself so foul a thing!—   45
And I was glad for Calderon. . . .
My God! if he could hear her sing
Just once, as I do!—There! she's done. . . .

No, it was only something wrong
A minute—something in my head.—   50
God, no!—she'll never stop that song
As long as I'm alive or dead!
As long as I am here or there,
She'll sing to me, a murderer!—
Well, I suppose the gods are fair. . . .   55
I killed her . . . Yes, I poisoned her!

But you, Francisco,—you are young;—
So take my hand and hear me, now:—
There are no lies upon your tongue,
There is no guilt upon your brow.—   60
But there is blood upon your name?—
And blood, you say, will rust the steel
That strikes for honor or for shame? . . .
Francisco, it is fear you feel!—

And such a miserable fear   65
That you, my boy, will call it pride;—
But you will grope from year to year
Until at last the clouds divide,
And all at once you meet the truth,
And curse yourself, with helpless rage,   70
For something you have lost with youth
And found again, too late, with age.

The truth, my brother, is just this:—
Your title here is nothing more
Or less than what your courage is: 75
The man must put himself before
The name, and once the master stay
Forever—or forever fall.—
Good-bye!—Remember what I say . . .
Good-bye!—Good-bye! . . . And that was all.   80

The lips were still: the man was dead.—
Francisco, with a weird surprise,
Stood like a stranger by the bed,
And there were no tears in his eyes.
But in his heart there was a grief   85
Too strong for human tears to free,—
And in his hand a written leaf
For Calderon across the sea.

JOHN EVERELDOWN

"Where are you going to-night, to-night,—
    Where are you going, John Evereldown?
There's never the sign of a star in sight,
    Nor a lamp that's nearer than Tilbury Town.
Why do you stare as a dead man might?   5
Where are you pointing away from the light?
And where are you going to-night, to-night,—
    Where are you going, John Evereldown?"

"Right through the forest, where none can see,
    There's where I'm going, to Tilbury Town.   10
The men are asleep,—or awake, may be,—
    But the women are calling John Evereldown.
Ever and ever they call for me,
And while they call can a man be free?
So right through the forest, where none can see, 15
    There's where I'm going, to Tilbury Town."

"But why are you going so late, so late,—
    Why are you going, John Evereldown?
Though the road be smooth and the path be straight,
    There are two long leagues to Tilbury Town. 20
Come in by the fire, old man, and wait!

Why do you chatter out there by the gate?
And why are you going so late, so late,—
 Why are you going, John Evereldown?"

"I follow the women wherever they call,—   25
 That's why I'm going to Tilbury Town.
God knows if I pray to be done with it all,
 But God is no friend to John Evereldown.
So the clouds may come and the rain may fall,
The shadows may creep and the dead men crawl,—   30
But I follow the women wherever they call,
 And that's why I'm going to Tilbury Town."

THE WORLD

Some are the brothers of all humankind,
 And own them, whatsoever their estate;
And some, for sorrow and self-scorn, are blind
 With enmity for man's unguarded fate.

For some there is a music all day long   5
 Like flutes in Paradise, they are so glad;
And there is hell's eternal under-song
 Of curses and the cries of men gone mad.

Some say the Scheme with love stands luminous,
 Some say 'twere better back to chaos hurled;   10
And so 'tis what we are that makes for us
 The measure and the meaning of the world.

CREDO

I cannot find my way: there is no star
In all the shrouded heavens anywhere;

And there is not a whisper in the air
Of any living voice but one so far
That I can hear it only as a bar   5
Of lost, imperial music, played when fair
And angel fingers wove, and unaware,
Dead leaves to garlands where no roses are.

No, there is not a glimmer, nor a call,
For one that welcomes, welcomes when he fears,   10
The black and awful chaos of the night;
For through it all,—above, beyond it all,—
I know the far-sent message of the years,
I feel the coming glory of the Light!

THE CHILDREN OF THE NIGHT

For those that never know the light,
   The darkness is a sullen thing;
And they, the Children of the Night,
   Seem lost in Fortune's winnowing.

But some are strong and some are weak,—   5
   And there's the story. House and home
Are shut from countless hearts that seek
   World-refuge that will never come.

And if there be no other life,
   And if there be no other chance   10
To weigh their sorrow and their strife
   Than in the scales of circumstance,

'Twere better, ere the sun go down
   Upon the first day we embark,
In life's imbittered sea to drown,   15
   Than sail forever in the dark.

But if there be a soul on earth
   So blinded with its own misuse
Of man's revealed, incessant worth,
   Or worn with anguish, that it views   20

No light but for a mortal eye,
   No rest but of a mortal sleep,
No God but in a prophet's lie,
   No faith for "honest doubt" to keep;

If there be nothing, good or bad,   25
   But chaos for a soul to trust,—
God counts it for a soul gone mad,
   And if God be God, He is just.

And if God be God, He is Love;
   And though the Dawn be still so dim,   30
It shows us we have played enough
   With creeds that make a fiend of Him.

There is one creed, and only one,
   That glorifies God's excellence;
So cherish, that His will be done,   35
   The common creed of common sense.

It is the crimson, not the gray,
   That charms the twilight of all time;
It is the promise of the day
   That makes the starry sky sublime;   40

It is the faith within the fear
   That holds us to the life we curse;—
So let us in ourselves revere
   The Self which is the Universe!

Let us, the Children of the Night,   45
    Put off the cloak that hides the scar!
Let us be Children of the Light,
    And tell the ages what we are!

THE CLERKS

I did not think that I should find them there
When I came back again; but there they stood,
As in the days they dreamed of when young blood
Was in their cheeks and women called them fair.
Be sure, they met me with an ancient air,—   5
And yes, there was a shop-worn brotherhood
About them; but the men were just as good,
And just as human as they ever were.

And you that ache so much to be sublime,
And you that feed yourselves with your descent,   10
What comes of all your visions and your fears?
Poets and kings are but the clerks of Time,
Tiering the same dull webs of discontent,
Clipping the same sad alnage of the years.

BALLADE BY THE FIRE

Slowly I smoke and hug my knee,
    The while a witless masquerade
Of things that only children see
    Floats in a mist of light and shade:
    They pass, a flimsy cavalcade,   5
And with a weak, remindful glow,
    The falling embers break and fade,
As one by one the phantoms go.

Then, with a melancholy glee
  To think where once my fancy strayed,   10
I muse on what the years may be
  Whose coming tales are all unsaid,
  Till tongs and shovel, snugly laid
Within their shadowed niches, grow
  By grim degrees to pick and spade,   15
As one by one the phantoms go.

But then, what though the mystic Three
  Around me ply their merry trade?—
And Charon soon may carry me
  Across the gloomy Stygian glade?—   20
  Be up, my soul! nor be afraid
Of what some unborn year may show;
  But mind your human debts are paid,
As one by one the phantoms go.

ENVOY

Life is the game that must be played: 25
  This truth at least, good friend, we know;
So live and laugh, nor be dismayed
  As one by one the phantoms go.

ON THE NIGHT OF A FRIEND'S WEDDING

If ever I am old, and all alone,
I shall have killed one grief, at any rate;
For then, thank God, I shall not have to wait
Much longer for the sheaves that I have sown.
The devil only knows what I have done,   5
But here I am, and here are six or eight
Good friends, who most ingenuously prate
About my songs to such and such a one.

But everything is all askew to-night,—
As if the time were come, or almost come,   10
For their untenanted mirage of me
To lose itself and crumble out of sight,
Like a tall ship that floats above the foam
A little while, and then breaks utterly.

VERLAINE

Why do you dig like long-clawed scavengers
To touch the covered corpse of him that fled
The uplands for the fens, and rioted
Like a sick satyr with doom's worshippers?
Come! let the grass grow there; and leave his verse   5
To tell the story of the life he led.
Let the man go: let the dead flesh be dead,
And let the worms be its biographers.

Song sloughs away the sin to find redress
In art's complete remembrance: nothing clings   10
For long but laurel to the stricken brow
That felt the Muse's finger; nothing less
Than hell's fulfilment of the end of things
Can blot the star that shines on Paris now.

THE GARDEN

There is a fenceless garden overgrown
With buds and blossoms and all sorts of leaves;
And once, among the roses and the sheaves,

The Gardener and I were there alone.
He led me to the plot where I had thrown   5
The fennel of my days on wasted ground,
And in that riot of sad weeds I found
The fruitage of a life that was my own.

My life! Ah, yes, there was my life, indeed!
And there were all the lives of humankind;   10
And they were like a book that I could read,
Whose every leaf, miraculously signed,
Outrolled itself from Thought's eternal seed,
Love-rooted in God's garden of the mind.

TWO SONNETS

I

Just as I wonder at the twofold screen
Of twisted innocence that you would plait
For eyes that uncourageously await
The coming of a kingdom that has been,
So do I wonder what God's love can mean   5
To you that all so strangely estimate
The purpose and the consequent estate
Of one short shuddering step to the Unseen.

No, I have not your backward faith to shrink
Lone-faring from the doorway of God's home   10
To find Him in the names of buried men;
Nor your ingenious recreance to think
We cherish, in the life that is to come,
The scattered features of dead friends again.

II

Never until our souls are strong enough
To plunge into the crater of the Scheme—
Triumphant in the flash there to redeem
Love's handsel and forevermore to slough,
Like cerements at a played-out masque, the rough   5
And reptile skins of us whereon we set
The stigma of scared years—are we to get
Where atoms and the ages are one stuff.

Nor ever shall we know the cursed waste
Of life in the beneficence divine   10
Of starlight and of sunlight and soul-shine
That we have squandered in sin's frail distress,
Till we have drunk, and trembled at the taste,
The mead of Thought's prophetic endlessness.

WALT WHITMAN

The master-songs are ended, and the man
That sang them is a name. And so is God
A name; and so is love, and life, and death,
And everything. But we, who are too blind
To read what we have written, or what faith   5
Has written for us, do not understand:
We only blink, and wonder.

Last night it was the song that was the man,
But now it is the man that is the song.
We do not hear him very much to-day: 10
His piercing and eternal cadence rings

Too pure for us—too powerfully pure,
Too lovingly triumphant, and too large;
But there are some that hear him, and they know
That he shall sing to-morrow for all men,   15
And that all time shall listen.

The master-songs are ended? Rather say
No songs are ended that are ever sung,
And that no names are dead names. When we write
Men's letters on proud marble or on sand,   20
We write them there forever.

KOSMOS

Ah,—shuddering men that falter and shrink so
To look on death,—what were the days we live,
Where life is half a struggle to forgive,
But for the love that finds us when we go?
Is God a jester? Does He laugh and throw   5
Poor branded wretches here to sweat and strive
For some vague end that never shall arrive?
And is He not yet weary of the show?

Think of it, all ye millions that have planned,
And only planned, the largess of hard youth!   10
Think of it, all ye builders on the sand,
Whose works are down!—Is love so small, forsooth?
Be brave! To-morrow you will understand
The doubt, the pain, the triumph, and the Truth!

AN OLD STORY

Strange that I did not know him then,
   That friend of mine!
I did not even show him then
   One friendly sign;

But cursed him for the ways he had   5
   To make me see
My envy of the praise he had
   For praising me.

I would have rid the earth of him
   Once, in my pride! . . .   10
I never knew the worth of him
   Until he died.

A POEM FOR MAX NORDAU

Dun shades quiver down the lone long fallow,
And the scared night shudders at the brown owl's cry;
The bleak reeds rattle as the winds whirl by,
The frayed leaves flutter through the clumped shrubs callow.

Chill dews clinging on the low cold mallow   5
Make a steel-keen shimmer where the spent stems lie;
Dun shades quiver down the lone long fallow,
And the scared night shudders at the brown owl's cry.

Pale stars peering through the clouds' curled shallow
Make a thin still flicker in a foul round sky;   10

Black damp shadows through the hushed air fly;
The lewd gloom wakens to a moon-sad sallow,
Dun shades quiver down the lone long fallow.

BOSTON

My northern pines are good enough for me,
But there's a town my memory uprears—
A town that always like a friend appears,
And always in the sunrise by the sea.
And over it, somehow, there seems to be
A downward flash of something new and fierce,
That ever strives to clear, but never clears
The dimness of a charmed antiquity.

I know my Boston is a counterfeit,—
A frameless imitation, all bereft
Of living nearness, noise, and common speech;
But I am glad for every glimpse of it,—
And there it is, plain as a name that's left
In letters by warm hands I cannot reach.

THE NIGHT BEFORE

Look you, Dominie; look you, and listen!
Look in my face, first; search every line there;
Mark every feature,—chin, lip, and forehead!
Look in my eyes, and tell me the lesson
You read there; measure my nose, and tell me
Where I am wanting! A man's nose, Dominie,
Is often the cast of his inward spirit;
So mark mine well. But why do you smile so?

Pity, or what? Is it written all over,
This face of mine, with a brute's confession? 10
Nothing but sin there? nothing but hell-scars?
Or is it because there is something better—
A glimmer of good, maybe—or a shadow
Of something that's followed me down from childhood—
Followed me all these years and kept me, 15
Spite of my slips and sins and follies,
Spite of my last red sin, my murder,—
Just out of hell? Yes? something of that kind?
And you smile for that? You're a good man, Dominie,
The one good man in the world who knows me,— 20
My one good friend in a world that mocks me,
Here in this hard stone cage. But I leave it
To-morrow. To-morrow! My God! am I crying?
Are these things tears? Tears! What! am I frightened?
I, who swore I should go to the scaffold 25
With big strong steps, and—No more. I thank you,
But no—I am all right now! No!—listen!
I am here to be hanged; to be hanged to-morrow
At six o'clock, when the sun is rising.
And why am I here? Not a soul can tell you 30
But this poor shivering thing before you,
This fluttering wreck of the man God made him,
For God knows what wild reason. Hear me,
And learn from my lips the truth of my story.
There's nothing strange in what I shall tell you, 35
Nothing mysterious, nothing unearthly,—
But damnably human,—and you shall hear it.
Not one of those little black lawyers had guessed it;
The judge, with his big bald head, never knew it;
And the jury (God rest their poor souls!) never dreamed it. 40
Once there were three in the world who could tell it;
Now there are two. There'll be two to-morrow,—
You, my friend, and—But there's the story:—

When I was a boy the world was heaven.
I never knew then that the men and the women
Who petted and called me a brave big fellow
Were ever less happy than I; but wisdom—
Which comes with the years, you know—soon showed me
The secret of all my glittering childhood,
The broken key to the fairies' castle
That held my life in the fresh, glad season
When I was the king of the earth. Then slowly—
And yet so swiftly!—there came the knowledge
That the marvellous life I had lived was my life;
That the glorious world I had loved was my world;
And that every man, and every woman,
And every child was a different being,
Wrought with a different heat, and fired
With passions born of a single spirit;
That the pleasure I felt was not their pleasure,
Nor my sorrow—a kind of nameless pity
For something, I knew not what—their sorrow.
And thus was I taught my first hard lesson,—
The lesson we suffer the most in learning:
That a happy man is a man forgetful
Of all the torturing ills around him.
When or where I first met the woman
I cherished and made my wife, no matter.
Enough to say that I found her and kept her
Here in my heart with as pure a devotion
As ever Christ felt for his brothers. Forgive me
For naming His name in your patient presence;
But I feel my words, and the truth I utter
Is God's own truth. I loved that woman,—
Not for her face, but for something fairer,
Something diviner, I thought, than beauty:
I loved the spirit—the human something
That seemed to chime with my own condition,
And make soul-music when we were together;

45

50

55

60

65

70

75

And we were never apart, from the moment   80
My eyes flashed into her eyes the message
That swept itself in a quivering answer
Back through my strange lost being. My pulses
Leapt with an aching speed; and the measure
Of this great world grew small and smaller,   85
Till it seemed the sky and the land and the ocean
Closed at last in a mist all golden
Around us two. And we stood for a season
Like gods outflung from chaos, dreaming
That we were the king and the queen of the fire   90
That reddened the clouds of love that held us
Blind to the new world soon to be ours—
Ours to seize and sway. The passion
Of that great love was a nameless passion,
Bright as the blaze of the sun at noonday,   95
Wild as the flames of hell; but, mark you,
Never a whit less pure for its fervor.
The baseness in me (for I was human)
Burned like a worm, and perished; and nothing
Was left me then but a soul that mingled   100
Itself with hers, and swayed and shuddered
In fearful triumph. When I consider
That helpless love and the cursed folly
That wrecked my life for the sake of a woman
Who broke with a laugh the chains of her marriage   105
(Whatever the word may mean), I wonder
If all the woe was her sin, or whether
The chains themselves were enough to lead her
In love's despite to break them. . . . Sinners
And saints—I say—are rocked in the cradle,   110
But never are known till the will within them
Speaks in its own good time. So I foster
Even to-night for the woman who wronged me,
Nothing of hate, nor of love, but a feeling

Of still regret; for the man—But hear me,   115
And judge for yourself:—

        For a time the seasons
Changed and passed in a sweet succession
That seemed to me like an endless music:
Life was a rolling psalm, and the choirs
Of God were glad for our love. I fancied   120
All this, and more than I dare to tell you
To-night,—yes, more than I dare to remember;
And then—well, the music stopped. There are moments
In all men's lives when it stops, I fancy,—
Or seems to stop,—till it comes to cheer them   125
Again with a larger sound. The curtain
Of life just then is lifted a little
To give to their sight new joys—new sorrows—
Or nothing at all, sometimes. I was watching
The slow, sweet scenes of a golden picture,   130
Flushed and alive with a long delusion
That made the murmur of home, when I shuddered
And felt like a knife that awful silence
That comes when the music goes—forever.
The truth came over my life like a darkness   135
Over a forest where one man wanders,
Worse than alone. For a time I staggered
And stumbled on with a weak persistence
After the phantom of hope that darted
And dodged like a frightened thing before me,   140
To quit me at last, and vanish. Nothing
Was left me then but the curse of living
And bearing through all my days the fever
And thirst of a poisoned love. Were I stronger,
Or weaker, perhaps my scorn had saved me,   145
Given me strength to crush my sorrow
With hate for her and the world that praised her—

To have left her, then and there—to have conquered
That old false life with a new and a wiser,—
Such things are easy in words. You listen,   150
And frown, I suppose, that I never mention
That beautiful word, *forgive!*—I forgave her
First of all; and I praised kind Heaven
That I was a brave, clean man to do it;
And then I tried to forget. Forgiveness!   155
What does it mean when the one forgiven
Shivers and weeps and clings and kisses
The credulous fool that holds her, and tells him
A thousand things of a good man's mercy,
And then slips off with a laugh and plunges   160
Back to the sin she has quit for a season,
To tell him that hell and the world are better
For her than a prophet's heaven? Believe me,
The love that dies ere its flames are wasted
In search of an alien soul is better,   165
Better by far than the lonely passion
That burns back into the heart that feeds it.
For I loved her still, and the more she mocked me,—
Fooled with her endless pleading promise
Of future faith,—the more I believed her   170
The penitent thing she seemed; and the stronger
Her choking arms and her small hot kisses
Bound me and burned my brain to pity,
The more she grew to the heavenly creature
That brightened the life I had lost forever.   175
The truth was gone somehow for the moment;
The curtain fell for a time; and I fancied
We were again like gods together,
Loving again with the old glad rapture.
But scenes like these, too often repeated,   180
Failed at last, and her guile was wasted.
I made an end of her shrewd caresses

And told her a few straight words. She took them
Full at their worth—and the farce was over.

. . . .

At first my dreams of the past upheld me,   185
But they were a short support: the present
Pushed them away, and I fell. The mission
Of life (whatever it was) was blasted;
My game was lost. And I met the winner
Of that foul deal as a sick slave gathers   190
His painful strength at the sight of his master;
And when he was past I cursed him, fearful
Of that strange chance which makes us mighty
Or mean, or both. I cursed him and hated
The stones he pressed with his heel; I followed   195
His easy march with a backward envy,
And cursed myself for the beast within me.
But pride is the master of love, and the vision
Of those old days grew faint and fainter:
The counterfeit wife my mercy sheltered   200
Was nothing now but a woman,—a woman
Out of my way and out of my nature.
My battle with blinded love was over,
My battle with aching pride beginning.
If I was the loser at first, I wonder   205
If I am the winner now! . . . I doubt it.
My life is a losing game; and to-morrow—
To-morrow!—Christ! did I say to-morrow? . . .
Is your brandy good for death? . . . There,—listen:—

When love goes out, and a man is driven   210
To shun mankind for the scars that make him
A joke for all chattering tongues, he carries
A double burden. The woes I suffered
After that hard betrayal made me

Pity, at first, all breathing creatures   215
On this bewildered earth. I studied
Their faces and made for myself the story
Of all their scattered lives. Like brothers
And sisters they seemed to me then; and I nourished
A stranger friendship wrought in my fancy   220
Between those people and me. But somehow,
As time went on, there came queer glances
Out of their eyes, and the shame that stung me
Harassed my pride with a crazed impression
That every face in the surging city   225
Was turned to me; and I saw sly whispers,
Now and then, as I walked and wearied
My wasted life twice over in bearing
With all my sorrow the sorrows of others,—
Till I found myself their fool. Then I trembled,—   230
A poor scared thing,—and their prying faces
Told me the ghastly truth: they were laughing
At me and my fate. My God, I could feel it—
That laughter! And then the children caught it;
And I, like a struck dog, crept and listened.   235
And then when I met the man who had weakened
A woman's love to his own desire,
It seemed to me that all hell were laughing
In fiendish concert! I was their victim—
And his, and hate's. And there was the struggle!   240
As long as the earth we tread holds something
A tortured heart can love, the meaning
Of life is not wholly blurred; but after
The last loved thing in the world has left us,
We know the triumph of hate. The glory   245
Of good goes out forever; the beacon
Of sin is the light that leads us downward—
Down to the fiery end. The road runs
Right through hell; and the souls that follow

The cursed ways where its windings lead them 250
Suffer enough, I say, to merit
All grace that a God can give.—The fashion
Of our belief is to lift all beings
Born for a life that knows no struggle
In sin's tight snares to eternal glory— 255
All apart from the branded millions
Who carry through life their faces graven
With sure brute scars that tell the story
Of their foul, fated passions. Science
Has yet no salve to smooth or soften 260
The cradle-scars of a tyrant's visage;
No drug to purge from the vital essence
Of souls the sleeping venom. Virtue
May flower in hell, when its roots are twisted
And wound with the roots of vice; but the stronger 265
Never is known till there comes that battle
With sin to prove the victor. Perilous
Things are these demons we call our passions:
Slaves are we of their roving fancies,
Fools of their devilish glee.—You think me, 270
I know, in this maundering way designing
To lighten the load of my guilt and cast it
Half on the shoulders of God. But hear me!
I'm partly a man,—for all my weakness,—
If weakness it were to stand and murder 275
Before men's eyes the man who had murdered
Me, and driven my burning forehead
With horns for the world to laugh at. Trust me!
And try to believe my words but a portion
Of what God's purpose made me! The coward 280
Within me cries for this; and I beg you
Now, as I come to the end, to remember
That women and men are on earth to travel
All on a different road. Hereafter

The roads may meet. . . . I trust in something—   285
I know not what. . . .

              Well, this was the way of it:—
Stung with the shame and the secret fury
That comes to the man who has thrown his pittance
Of self at a traitor's feet, I wandered
Weeks and weeks in a baffled frenzy,   290
Till at last the devil spoke. I heard him,
And laughed at the love that strove to touch me,—
The dead, lost love; and I gripped the demon
Close to my breast, and held him, praising
The fates and the furies that gave me the courage   295
To follow his wild command. Forgetful
Of all to come when the work was over,—
There came to me then no stony vision
Of these three hundred days,—I cherished
An awful joy in my brain. I pondered   300
And weighed the thing in my mind, and gloried
In life to think that I was to conquer
Death at his own dark door,—and chuckled
To think of it done so cleanly. One evening
I knew that my time had come. I shuddered   305
A little, but rather for doubt than terror,
And followed him,—led by the nameless devil
I worshipped and called my brother. The city
Shone like a dream that night; the windows
Flashed with a piercing flame, and the pavements   310
Pulsed and swayed with a warmth—or something
That seemed so then to my feet—and thrilled me
With a quick, dizzy joy; and the women
And men, like marvellous things of magic,
Floated and laughed and sang by my shoulder,   315
Sent with a wizard motion. Through it
And over and under it all there sounded
A murmur of life, like bees; and I listened

And laughed again to think of the flower
That grew, blood-red, for me! . . . This fellow   320
Was one of the popular sort who flourish
Unruffled where gods would fall. For a conscience
He carried a snug deceit that made him
The man of the time and the place, whatever
The time or the place might be. Were he sounding,   325
With a genial craft that cloaked its purpose,
Nigh to itself, the depth of a woman
Fooled with his brainless art, or sending
The midnight home with songs and bottles,—
The cad was there, and his ease forever   330
Shone with the smooth and slippery polish
That tells the snake. That night he drifted
Into an up-town haunt and ordered—
Whatever it was—with a soft assurance
That made me mad as I stood behind him,   335
Gripping his death, and waited. Coward,
I think, is the name the world has given
To men like me; but I'll swear I never
Thought of my own disgrace when I shot him—
Yes, in the back,—I know it, I know it   340
Now; but what if I do? . . . As I watched him
Lying there dead in the scattered sawdust,
Wet with a day's blown froth, I noted
That things were still; that the walnut tables,
Where men but a moment before were sitting,   345
Were gone; that a screen of something around me
Shut them out of my sight. But the gilded
Signs of a hundred beers and whiskeys
Flashed from the walls above, and the mirrors
And glasses behind the bar were lighted   350
In some strange way, and into my spirit
A thousand shafts of terrible fire
Burned like death, and I fell. The story
Of what came then, you know.

But tell me,
What does the whole thing mean? What are we,—   355
Slaves of an awful ignorance? puppets
Pulled by a fiend? or gods, without knowing it?
Do we shut from ourselves our own salvation,—
Or what do we do! I tell you, Dominie,
There are times in the lives of us poor devils   360
When heaven and hell get mixed. Though conscience
May come like a whisper of Christ to warn us
Away from our sins, it is lost or laughed at,—
And then we fall. And for all who have fallen—
Even for him—I hold no malice,   365
Nor much compassion: a mightier mercy
Than mine must shrive him.—And I—I am going
Into the light?—or into the darkness?
Why do I sit through these sickening hours,
And hope? Good God! are they hours?—hours?   370
Yes! I am done with days. And to-morrow—
We two may meet! To-morrow!—To-morrow! . . .

TWO MEN

There be two men of all mankind
    That I should like to know about;
But search and question where I will,
    I cannot ever find them out.

Melchizedek he praised the Lord,   5
    And gave some wine to Abraham;
But who can tell what else he did
    Must be more learned than I am.

Ucalegon he lost his house
    When Agamemnon came to Troy;   10
But who can tell me who he was—
    I'll pray the gods to give him joy.

There be two men of all mankind
    That I'm forever thinking on:
They chase me everywhere I go,—   15
    Melchizedek, Ucalegon.

RICHARD CORY

Whenever Richard Cory went down town,
We people on the pavement looked at him:
He was a gentleman from sole to crown,
Clean favored, and imperially slim.

And he was always quietly arrayed,   5
And he was always human when he talked;
But still he fluttered pulses when he said,
"Good-morning," and he glittered when he walked.

And he was rich,—yes, richer than a king,—
And admirably schooled in every grace: 10
In fine, we thought that he was everything
To make us wish that we were in his place.

So on we worked, and waited for the light,
And went without the meat, and cursed the bread;
And Richard Cory, one calm summer night,   15
Went home and put a bullet through his head.

TWO OCTAVES

I

Not by the grief that stuns and overwhelms
All outward recognition of revealed
And righteous omnipresence are the days
Of most of us affrighted and diseased,
But rather by the common snarls of life   5
That come to test us and to strengthen us
In this the prentice-age of discontent,
Rebelliousness, faint-heartedness, and shame.

II

When through hot fog the fulgid sun looks down
Upon a stagnant earth where listless men
Laboriously dawdle, curse, and sweat,
Disqualified, unsatisfied, inert,—
It seems to me somehow that God himself   5
Scans with a close reproach what I have done,
Counts with an unphrased patience my arrears,
And fathoms my unprofitable thoughts.

CALVARY

Friendless and faint, with martyred steps and slow,
Faint for the flesh, but for the spirit free,
Stung by the mob that came to see the show,
The Master toiled along to Calvary;
We gibed him, as he went, with houndish glee,   5
Till his dimmed eyes for us did overflow;
We cursed his vengeless hands thrice wretchedly,—
And this was nineteen hundred years ago.

But after nineteen hundred years the shame
Still clings, and we have not made good the loss   10
That outraged faith has entered in his name.
Ah, when shall come love's courage to be strong!
Tell me, O Lord—tell me, O Lord, how long
Are we to keep Christ writhing on the cross!

THE STORY OF THE ASHES AND THE FLAME

No matter why, nor whence, nor when she came,
There was her place. No matter what men said,
No matter what she was; living or dead,
Faithful or not, he loved her all the same.
The story was as old as human shame,   5
But ever since that lonely night she fled,
With books to blind him, he had only read
The story of the ashes and the flame.

There she was always coming pretty soon
To fool him back, with penitent scared eyes   10
That had in them the laughter of the moon
For baffled lovers, and to make him think—
Before she gave him time enough to wink—
Sin's kisses were the keys to Paradise.

AMARYLLIS

Once, when I wandered in the woods alone,
An old man tottered up to me and said,
"Come, friend, and see the grave that I have made
For Amaryllis." There was in the tone

Of his complaint such quaver and such moan   5
That I took pity on him and obeyed,
And long stood looking where his hands had laid
An ancient woman, shrunk to skin and bone.

Far out beyond the forest I could hear
The calling of loud progress, and the bold   10
Incessant scream of commerce ringing clear;
But though the trumpets of the world were glad,
It made me lonely and it made me sad
To think that Amaryllis had grown old.

THE PITY OF THE LEAVES

Vengeful across the cold November moors,
Loud with ancestral shame there came the bleak
Sad wind that shrieked, and answered with a shriek,
Reverberant through lonely corridors.
The old man heard it; and he heard, perforce,   5
Words out of lips that were no more to speak—
Words of the past that shook the old man's cheek
Like dead, remembered footsteps on old floors.

And then there were the leaves that plagued him so!
The brown, thin leaves that on the stones outside   10
Skipped with a freezing whisper. Now and then
They stopped, and stayed there—just to let him know
How dead they were; but if the old man cried,
They fluttered off like withered souls of men.

CLIFF KLINGENHAGEN

Cliff Klingenhagen had me in to dine
With him one day; and after soup and meat,
And all the other things there were to eat,
Cliff took two glasses and filled one with wine
And one with wormwood. Then, without a sign   5
For me to choose at all, he took the draught
Of bitterness himself, and lightly quaffed
It off, and said the other one was mine.

And when I asked him what the deuce he meant
By doing that, he only looked at me   10
And grinned, and said it was a way of his.
And though I know the fellow, I have spent
Long time a-wondering when I shall be
As happy as Cliff Klingenhagen is.

CHARLES CARVILLE'S EYES

A melancholy face Charles Carville had,
But not so melancholy as it seemed,—
When once you knew him,—for his mouth redeemed
His insufficient eyes, forever sad:
In them there was no life-glimpse, good or bad,—   5
Nor joy nor passion in them ever gleamed;
His mouth was all of him that ever beamed,
His eyes were sorry, but his mouth was glad.

He never was a fellow that said much,
And half of what he did say was not heard   10

By many of us: we were out of touch
With all his whims and all his theories
Till he was dead, so those blank eyes of his
Might speak them. Then we heard them, every word.

FLEMING HELPHENSTINE

At first I thought there was a superfine
Persuasion in his face; but the free glow
That filled it when he stopped and cried, "Hollo!"
Shone joyously, and so I let it shine.
He said his name was Fleming Helphenstine,   5
But be that as it may;—I only know
He talked of this and that and So-and-So,
And laughed and chaffed like any friend of mine.

But soon, with a queer, quick frown, he looked at me,
And I looked hard at him; and there we gazed   10
With a strained shame that made us cringe and wince:
Then, with a wordless clogged apology
That sounded half confused and half amazed,
He dodged,—and I have never seen him since.

REUBEN BRIGHT

Because he was a butcher and thereby
Did earn an honest living (and did right),
I would not have you think that Reuben Bright
Was any more a brute than you or I;
For when they told him that his wife must die,
He stared at them, and shook with grief and fright,
And cried like a great baby half that night,
And made the women cry to see him cry.

And after she was dead, and he had paid
The singers and the sexton and the rest,   10
He packed a lot of things that she had made
Most mournfully away in an old chest
Of hers, and put some chopped-up cedar boughs
In with them, and tore down the slaughter-house.

THE TAVERN

Whenever I go by there nowadays
And look at the rank weeds and the strange grass,
The torn blue curtains and the broken glass,
I seem to be afraid of the old place;
And something stiffens up and down my face,   5
For all the world as if I saw the ghost
Of old Ham Amory, the murdered host,
With his dead eyes turned on me all aglaze.

The Tavern has a story, but no man
Can tell us what it is. We only know   10
That once long after midnight, years ago,
A stranger galloped up from Tilbury Town,
Who brushed, and scared, and all but overran
That skirt-crazed reprobate, John Evereldown.

OCTAVES

I

To get at the eternal strength of things,
And fearlessly to make strong songs of it,
Is, to my mind, the mission of that man
The world would call a poet. He may sing

But roughly, and withal ungraciously;   5
But if he touch to life the one right chord
Wherein God's music slumbers, and awake
To truth one drowsed ambition, he sings well.

II

We thrill too strangely at the master's touch;
We shrink too sadly from the larger self
Which for its own completeness agitates
And undetermines us; we do not feel—
We dare not feel it yet—the splendid shame   5
Of uncreated failure; we forget,
The while we groan, that God's accomplishment
Is always and unfailingly at hand.

III

To mortal ears the plainest word may ring
Fantastic and unheard-of, and as false
And out of tune as ever to our own
Did ring the prayers of man-made maniacs;
But if that word be the plain word of Truth,   5
It leaves an echo that begets itself,
Persistent in itself and of itself,
Regenerate, reiterate, replete.

IV

Tumultuously void of a clean scheme
Whereon to build, whereof to formulate,
The legion life that riots in mankind
Goes ever plunging upward, up and down,
Most like some crazy regiment at arms,   5
Undisciplined of aught but Ignorance,
And ever led resourcelessly along
To brainless carnage by drunk trumpeters

V

To me the groaning of world-worshippers
Rings like a lonely music played in hell
By one with art enough to cleave the walls
Of heaven with his cadence, but without
The wisdom or the will to comprehend   5
The strangeness of his own perversity,
And all without the courage to deny
The profit and the pride of his defeat.

VI

While we are drilled in error, we are lost
Alike to truth and usefulness. We think
We are great warriors now, and we can brag
Like Titans; but the world is growing young,
And we, the fools of time, are growing with it:—   5
We do not fight to-day, we only die;
We are too proud of death, and too ashamed
Of God, to know enough to be alive.

VII

There is one battle-field whereon we fall
Triumphant and unconquered; but, alas!
We are too fleshly fearful of ourselves
To fight there till our days are whirled and blurred
By sorrow, and the ministering wheels   5
Of anguish take us eastward, where the clouds
Of human gloom are lost against the gleam
That shines on Thought's impenetrable mail.

VIII

When we shall hear no more the cradle-songs
Of ages—when the timeless hymns of Love
Defeat them and outsound them—we shall know
The rapture of that large release which all

Right science comprehends; and we shall read,   5
With unoppressed and unoffended eyes,
That record of All-Soul whereon God writes
In everlasting runes the truth of Him.

IX

The guerdon of new childhood is repose:—
Once he has read the primer of right thought,
A man may claim between two smithy strokes
Beatitude enough to realize
God's parallel completeness in the vague   5
And incommensurable excellence
That equitably uncreates itself
And makes a whirlwind of the Universe.

X

There is no loneliness:—no matter where
We go, nor whence we come, nor what good friends
Forsake us in the seeming, we are all
At one with a complete companionship;
And though forlornly joyless be the ways   5
We travel, the compensate spirit-gleams
Of Wisdom shaft the darkness here and there,
Like scattered lamps in unfrequented streets.

XI

When one that you and I had all but sworn
To be the purest thing God ever made
Bewilders us until at last it seems
An angel has come back restigmatized,—
Faith wavers, and we wonder what there is   5
On earth to make us faithful any more,
But never are quite wise enough to know
The wisdom that is in that wonderment.

XII

Where does a dead man go?—The dead man dies;
But the free life that would no longer feed
On fagots of outburned and shattered flesh
Wakes to a thrilled invisible advance,
Unchained (or fettered else) of memory;   5
And when the dead man goes it seems to me
'T were better for us all to do away
With weeping, and be glad that he is gone.

XIII

Still through the dusk of dead, blank-legended,
And unremunerative years we search
To get where life begins, and still we groan
Because we do not find the living spark
Where no spark ever was; and thus we die,   5
Still searching, like poor old astronomers
Who totter off to bed and go to sleep,
To dream of untriangulated stars.

XIV

With conscious eyes not yet sincere enough
To pierce the glimmered cloud that fluctuates
Between me and the glorifying light
That screens itself with knowledge, I discern
The searching rays of wisdom that reach through   5
The mist of shame's infirm credulity,
And infinitely wonder if hard words
Like mine have any message for the dead.

XV

I grant you friendship is a royal thing,
But none shall ever know that royalty
For what it is till he has realized

His best friend in himself. 'T is then, perforce,
That man's unfettered faith indemnifies   5
Of its own conscious freedom the old shame,
And love's revealed infinitude supplants
Of its own wealth and wisdom the old scorn.

XVI

Though the sick beast infect us, we are fraught
Forever with indissoluble Truth,
Wherein redress reveals itself divine,
Transitional, transcendent. Grief and loss,
Disease and desolation, are the dreams   5
Of wasted excellence; and every dream
Has in it something of an ageless fact
That flouts deformity and laughs at years.

XVII

We lack the courage to be where we are:—
We love too much to travel on old roads,
To triumph on old fields; we love too much
To consecrate the magic of dead things,
And yielding to linger by long walls   5
Of ruin, where the ruinous moonlight
That sheds a lying glory on old stones
Befriends us with a wizard's enmity.

XVIII

Something as one with eyes that look below
The battle-smoke to glimpse the foeman's charge,
We through the dust of downward years may scan
The onslaught that awaits this idiot world
Where blood pays blood for nothing, and where life   5
Pays life to madness, till at last the ports
Of gilded helplessness be battered through
By the still crash of salvatory steel.

XIX

To you that sit with Sorrow like chained slaves,
And wonder if the night will ever come,
I would say this: The night will never come,
And sorrow is not always. But my words
Are not enough; your eyes are not enough;   5
The soul itself must insulate the Real,
Or ever you do cherish in this life—
In this life or in any life—repose.

XX

Like a white wall whereon forever breaks
Unsatisfied the tumult of green seas,
Man's unconjectured godliness rebukes
With its imperial silence the lost waves
Of insufficient grief. This mortal surge   5
That beats against us now is nothing else
Than plangent ignorance. Truth neither shakes
Nor wavers; but the world shakes, and we shriek.

XXI

Nor jewelled phrase nor mere mellifluous rhyme
Reverberates aright, or ever shall,
One cadence of that infinite plain-song
Which is itself all music. Stronger notes
Than any that have ever touched the world   5
Must ring to tell it—ring like hammer-blows,
Right-echoed of a chime primordial,
On anvils, in the gleaming of God's forge.

XXII

The prophet of dead words defeats himself:
Whoever would acknowledge and include
The foregleam and the glory of the real,
Must work with something else than pen and ink

And painful preparation: he must work 5
With unseen implements that have no names,
And he must win withal, to do that work,
Good fortitude, clean wisdom, and strong skill.

XXIII

To curse the chilled insistence of the dawn
Because the free gleam lingers; to defraud
The constant opportunity that lives
Unchallenged in all sorrow; to forget
For this large prodigality of gold 5
That larger generosity of thought,—
These are the fleshly clogs of human greed,
The fundamental blunders of mankind.

XXIV

Forebodings are the fiends of Recreance;
The master of the moment, the clean seer
Of ages, too securely scans what is,
Ever to be appalled at what is not;
He sees beyond the groaning borough lines 5
Of Hell, God's highways gleaming, and he knows
That Love's complete communion is the end
Of anguish to the liberated man.

XXV

Here by the windy docks I stand alone,
But yet companioned. There the vessel goes,
And there my friend goes with it; but the wake
That melts and ebbs between that friend and me
Love's earnest is of Life's all-purposeful 5
And all-triumphant sailing, when the ships
Of Wisdom loose their fretful chains and swing
Forever from the crumbled wharves of Time.

TWO QUATRAINS

I

Unity

As eons of incalculable strife
Are in the vision of one moment caught,
So are the common, concrete things of life
Divinely shadowed on the walls of Thought.

II

Paraphrase

We shriek to live, but no man ever lives
Till he has rid the ghost of human breath;
We dream to die, but no man ever dies
Till he has quit the road that runs to death.

ROMANCE

I

Boys

We were all boys, and three of us were friends;
And we were more than friends, it seemed to me:—
Yes, we were more than brothers then, we three. . . .
Brothers? . . . But we were boys, and there it ends.

II

James Wetherell

We never half believed the stuff
They told about James Wetherell;
We always liked him well enough,
And always tried to use him well;
But now some things have come to light,   5
And James has vanished from our view,—
There isn't very much to write,
There isn't very much to do.

L'ENVOI

Now in a thought, now in a shadowed word,
Now in a voice that thrills eternity,
Ever there comes an onward phrase to me
Of some transcendent music I have heard;
No piteous thing by soft hands dulcimered,   5
No trumpet crash of blood-sick victory,
But a glad strain of some still symphony
That no proud mortal touch has ever stirred.

There is no music in the world like this,
No character wherewith to set it down,   10
No kind of instrument to make it sing.
No kind of instrument? Ah, yes, there is!
And after time and place are overthrown,
God's touch will keep its one chord quivering.

❦ ❦ ❦

CAPTAIN CRAIG:
A BOOK OF POEMS

CAPTAIN CRAIG

I

I doubt if ten men in all Tilbury Town
Had ever shaken hands with Captain Craig,
Or called him by his name, or looked at him
So curiously, or so concernedly,
As they had looked at ashes; but a few—   5
Say five or six of us—had found somehow
The spark in him, and we had fanned it there,
Choked under, like a jest in Holy Writ,
By Tilbury prudence. He had lived his life,
And he had shared, with all of humankind,   10
Inveterate leave to fashion of himself,
By some resplendent metamorphosis,
Whatever he was not. And after time,
When it had come sufficiently to pass
That he was going patch-clad through the streets,   15
Weak, dizzy, chilled, and half starved, he had laid
Some nerveless fingers on a prudent sleeve
And told the sleeve, in furtive confidence,
Just how it was: "My name is Captain Craig,"
He said, "and I must eat." The sleeve moved on,   20
And after it moved others—one or two;
For Captain Craig, before the day was done,
Got back to the scant refuge of his bed

And shivered into it without a curse—
Without a murmur even. He was cold,   25
And old, and hungry; but the worst of it
Was a forlorn familiar consciousness
That he had failed again. There was a time
When he had fancied, if worst came to worst,
And he could work no more, that he might beg   30
Nor be the less for it; but when it came
To practice he found out that he had not
The genius. It was that, and that was all:
Experience had made him to detect
The blunder for his own, like all the rest   35
Of him. There were no other men to blame.
He was himself, and he had lost the speed
He started with, and he was left behind.
There was no mystery, no tragedy;
And if they found him lying on his back   40
Stone dead there some sharp morning, as they might,—
Well, once upon a time there was a man—
Es war einmal ein König, if it pleased him.
And he was right: there were no men to blame:
There was just a false note in the Tilbury tune—   45
A note that able-bodied men might sound
Hosannas on while Captain Craig lay quiet.
They might have made him sing by feeding him
Till he should work again, but probably
Such yielding would have jeopardized the rhythm;   50
They found it more melodious to shout
Right on, with unmolested adoration,
To keep the tune as it had always been,
To trust in God, and let the Captain starve.

He must have understood that afterwards—   55
When we had laid some fuel to the spark
Of him, and oxidized it—for he laughed
Out loud and long at us to feel it burn,

And then, for gratitude, made game of us:
"You are the resurrection and the life,"   60
He said, "and I the hymn the Brahmin sings;
O Fuscus! and we'll go no more a-roving."

We were not quite accoutred for a blast
Of any lettered nonchalance like that,
And some of us—the five or six of us   65
Who found him out—were singularly struck.
But soon there came assurance of his lips,
Like phrases out of some sweet instrument
Man's hand had never fitted, that he felt
"No penitential shame for what had come,   70
No virtuous regret for what had been,—
But rather a joy to find it in his life
To be an outcast usher of the soul
For such as had good courage of the Sun
To pattern Love." The Captain had one chair;   75
And on the bottom of it, like a king,
For longer time than I dare chronicle,
Sat with an ancient ease and eulogized
His opportunity. My friends got out,
Like brokers out of Arcady; but I—   80
May be for fascination of the thing,
Or may be for the larger humor of it—
Stayed listening, unwearied and unstung.
When they were gone the Captain's tuneful ooze
Of rhetoric took on a change; he smiled   85
At me and then continued, earnestly:
"Your friends have had enough of it; but you,
For a motive hardly vindicated yet
By prudence or by conscience, have remained;
And that is very good, for I have things   90
To tell you: things that are not words alone
Which are the ghosts of things—but something firmer.
"First, would I have you know, for every gift

Or sacrifice, there are—or there may be—
Two kinds of gratitude: the sudden kind   95
We feel for what we take, the slower kind
We feel for what we give. Once we have learned
As much as this, we know the truth has been
Told over to the world a thousand times;—
But we have had no ears to listen yet   100
For more than fragments of it: we have heard
A murmur now and then, an echo here
And there, and we have made great music of it;
And we have made innumerable books
To please the Unknown God. Time throws away   105
Dead thousands of them, but the God that knows
No death denies not one: the books all count,
The songs all count; and yet God's music has
No modes, his language has no adjectives."

"You may be right, you may be wrong," said I;   110
"But what has all of this that you say now—
This nineteenth-century Nirvana-talk—
To do with you and me?" The Captain raised
His hand and held it westward, where a patched
And unwashed attic-window filtered in   115
What barren light could reach us, and then said,
With a suave, complacent resonance: "There shines
The sun. Behold it. We go round and round,
And wisdom comes to us with every whirl
We count throughout the circuit. We may say   120
The child is born, the boy becomes a man,
The man does this and that, and the man goes,—
But having said it we have not said much,
Not very much. Do I fancy, or you think,
That it will be the end of anything   125
When I am gone? There was a soldier once
Who fought one fight and in that fight fell dead.
Sad friends went after, and they brought him home

And had a brass band at his funeral,
As you should have at mine; and after that   130
A few remembered him. But he was dead,
They said, and they should have their friend no more.—
However, there was once a starveling child—
A ragged-vested little incubus,
Born to be cuffed and frighted out of all   135
Capacity for childhood's happiness—
Who started out one day, quite suddenly,
To drown himself. He ran away from home,
Across the clover-fields and through the woods,
And waited on the rock above the stream,   140
Just like a kingfisher. He might have dived,
Or jumped, or he might not; but anyhow,
There came along a man who looked at him
With such an unexpected friendliness,
And talked with him in such a common way,   145
That life grew marvelously different:
What he had lately known for sullen trunks
And branches, and a world of tedious leaves,
Was all transmuted; a faint forest wind
That once had made the loneliest of all   150
Sad sounds on earth, made now the rarest music;
And the water that had called him once to death
Now seemed a flowing glory. And that man,
Born to go down a soldier, did this thing.—
Not much to do? Not very much, I grant you: 155
Good occupation for a sonneteer,
Or for a clown, or for a clergyman,
But small work for a soldier. By the way,
When you are weary sometimes of your own
Utility, I wonder if you find   160
Occasional great comfort pondering
What power a man has in him to put forth?
'Of all the many marvelous things that are,
Nothing is there more marvelous than man,'

Said Sophocles; and he lived long ago;   165
'And earth, unending ancient of the gods
He furrows; and the ploughs go back and forth,
Turning the broken mould, year after year.' . . .

"I turned a little furrow of my own
Once on a time, and everybody laughed—   170
As I laughed afterwards; and I doubt not
The First Intelligence, which we have drawn
In our competitive humility
As if it went forever on two legs,
Had some diversion of it: I believe   175
God's humor is the music of the spheres—
But even as we draft omnipotence
Itself to our own image, we pervert
The courage of an infinite ideal
To finite resignation. You have made   180
The cement of your churches out of tears
And ashes, and the fabric will not stand:
The shifted walls that you have coaxed and shored
So long with unavailing compromise
Will crumble down to dust and blow away,   185
And younger dust will follow after them;
Though not the faintest or the farthest whirled
First atom of the least that ever flew
Shall be by man defrauded of the touch
God thrilled it with to make a dream for man   190
When Science was unborn. And after time,
When we have earned our spiritual ears,
And art's commiseration of the truth
No longer glorifies the singing beast,
Or venerates the clinquant charlatan,—   195
Then shall at last come ringing through the sun,
Through time, through flesh, God's music of the soul.
For wisdom is that music, and all joy
That wisdom:—you may counterfeit, you think,

The burden of it in a thousand ways;   200
But as the bitterness that loads your tears
Makes Dead Sea swimming easy, so the gloom,
The penance, and the woeful pride you keep,
Make bitterness your buoyance of the world.
And at the fairest and the frenziedest   205
Alike of your God-fearing festivals,
You so compound the truth to pamper fear
That in the doubtful surfeit of your faith
You clamor for the food that shadows eat.
You call it rapture or deliverance,—   210
Passion or exaltation, or what most
The moment needs, but your faint-heartedness
Lives in it yet: you quiver and you clutch
For something larger, something unfulfilled,
Some wiser kind of joy that you shall have   215
Never, until you learn to laugh with God."
And with a calm Socratic patronage,
At once half sombre and half humorous,
The Captain reverently twirled his thumbs
And fixed his eyes on something far away;   220
Then, with a gradual gaze, conclusive, shrewd,
And at the moment unendurable
For sheer beneficence, he looked at me.—
"But the brass band?" I said, not quite at ease
With altruism yet.—He made a kind   225
Of reminiscent little inward noise,
Midway between a chuckle and a laugh,
And that was all his answer: not a word
Of explanation or suggestion came
From those tight-smiling lips. And when I left,   230
I wondered, as I trod the creaking snow
And had the world-wide air to breathe again,—
Though I had seen the tremor of his mouth
And honored the endurance of his hand—
Whether or not, securely closeted   235

Up there in the stived haven of his den,
The man sat laughing at me; and I felt
My teeth grind hard together with a quaint
Revulsion—as I think back on it now—
Not only for my Captain, but as well   240
For every smug-faced failure on God's earth—
Albeit I could swear, at the same time,
That there were tears in the old fellow's eyes.
I question if in tremors or in tears
There be more guidance to man's worthiness   245
Than—well, say in his prayers. But oftentimes
It humors us to think that we possess
By some divine adjustment of our own
Particular shrewd cells, or something else,
What others, for untutored sympathy,   250
Go spirit-fishing more than half their lives
To catch—like cheerful sinners to catch faith;
And I have not a doubt but I assumed
Some egotistic attribute like this
When, cautiously, next morning I reduced   255
The fretful qualms of my novitiate,
For most part, to an undigested pride.
Only, I live convinced that I regret
This enterprise no more than I regret
My life; and I am glad that I was born.   260

That evening, at "The Chrysalis," I found
The faces of my comrades all suffused
With what I chose then to denominate
Superfluous good feeling. In return,
They loaded me with titles of odd form   265
And unexemplified significance,
Like "Bellows-mender to Prince Æolus,"
"Pipe-filler to the Hoboscholiast,"
"Bread-fruit for the Non-Doing," with one more
That I remember, and a dozen more   270

That I forget. I may have been disturbed,
I do not say that I was not annoyed,
But something of the same serenity
That fortified me later made me feel
For their skin-pricking arrows not so much   275
Of pain as of a vigorous defect
In this world's archery. I might have tried,
With a flat facetiousness, to demonstrate
What they had only snapped at and thereby
Made out of my best evidence no more   280
Than comfortable food for their conceit;
But patient wisdom frowned on argument,
With a side nod for silence, and I smoked
A series of incurable dry pipes
While Morgan fiddled, with obnoxious care,   285
Some things that I detested.—Killigrew,
Drowsed with a fond abstraction, like an ass,
Lay blinking at me while he grinned and made
Remarks. The learned Plunket made remarks.

It may have been for smoke that I cursed cats   290
That night, but I have rather to believe
As I lay turning, twisting, listening,
And wondering, between great sleepless yawns,
What possible satisfaction those dead leaves
Could find in sending shadows to my room   295
And swinging them like black rags on a line,
That I, with a forlorn clear-headedness
Was ekeing out probation. I had sinned
In fearing to believe what I believed,
And I was paying for it.—Whimsical,   300
You think,—factitious; but "there is no luck,
No fate, no fortune for us, but the old
Unswerving and inviolable price
Gets paid: God sells himself eternally,
But never gives a crust," my friend had said;   305

And while I watched those leaves, and heard those cats,
And with half mad minuteness analyzed
The Captain's attitude and then my own,
I felt at length as one who throws himself
Down restless on a couch when clouds are dark,   310
And shuts his eyes to find, when he wakes up
And opens them again, what seems at first
An unfamiliar sunlight in his room
And in his life—as if the child in him
Had laughed and let him see; and then I knew   315
Some prowling superfluity of child
In me had found the child in Captain Craig
And had the sunlight reach him. While I slept,
That thought reshaped itself to friendly dreams,
And in the morning it was with me still.   320

Through March and shifting April to the time
When winter first becomes a memory
My friend the Captain—to my other friend's
Incredulous regret that such as he
Should ever get the talons of his talk   325
So fixed in my unfledged credulity—
Kept up the peroration of his life,
Not yielding at a threshold, nor, I think,
Too often on the stairs. He made me laugh
Sometimes, and then again he made me weep   330
Almost; for I had insufficiency
Enough in me to make me know the truth
Within the jest, and I could feel it there
As well as if it were the folded note
I felt between my fingers. I had said   335
Before that I should have to go away
And leave him for the season; and his eyes
Had shone with well-becoming interest
At that intelligence. There was no mist
In them that I remember; but I marked   340

An unmistakable self-questioning
And a reticence of unassumed regret.
The two together made anxiety—
Not selfishness, I ventured. I should see
No more of him for six or seven months,   345
And I was there to tell him as I might
What humorous provision we had made
For keeping him locked up in Tilbury Town.
That finished—with a few more commonplace
Prosaics on the certified event   350
Of my return to find him young again—
I left him neither vexed, I thought, with us,
Nor very much at odds with destiny.
At any rate, save always for a look
That I had seen too often to mistake   355
Or to forget, he gave no other sign.

When I was in the street I heard him shout
Some anxious Latin down; but a slow load
Of trailing rails absorbed it, and I lost
Whatever of good counsel or farewell   360
It may have had for me. I turned about
And having waved a somewhat indistinct
Acknowledgement, I walked along. The train
Was late and I was early, but the gap
Was filled and even crowded. Killigrew   365
Had left his pigeonholes to say good-by,
And he stood waiting by the ticket window
Like one grin-cursed of Orcus.—"You have heard?"
Said he.—"Heard what?" said I.—"He! he!" said he;
"Then your gray-headed beneficiary—   370
Your paragon of abstract usefulness—
Your philhellenic proletariat—
He! he!"—"But what the devil is it all
About?" said I. "What has he done? What ails him?"—
"What has he done? Ye gods! What has he done?   375

Man, he's a tramp—a Waggles—a dead beat!
I have a friend who knew him fifteen years
Ago, and I have his assurance now
That your sequestered parasite achieved
The same discreet collapse, at intervals,   380
Then as when first you found him. And you ask
What he has done! Go find a looking-glass
And you may see some recent work of his—
The most remunerative, and I think
The most unconscious.
               With another man   385
I might have made of that last adjective
A stimulating text; but Killigrew
Was not the one for me to stimulate
In five defective minutes, and I knew it.
So I offer no defense for keeping still   390
While he gave birth to phrases for my sake,
Nor more for staring at the changeless curve
Where river and railroad vanished, half a mile
Beyond us to the north. I gave him leave
To talk as long as he had words in him,   395
And watched the track and waited for the train;
And I remember, when the brakes had ceased
Their welcome wheezing and the place was filled
With yells and shadows and official smash,
How he ground my patient fingers and said, "Well,   400
Good-by, old man!—good-by! And don't forget:
Patrician, but all Waggles to the grave."
The grin became a smile soon after that,
And I knew that he had let the Captain go;
And I could read, where once the jest had been,   405
The spirit of the friend who cared the most.

The train began to move; and as it moved,
I felt a comfortable sudden change
All over and inside. Partly it seemed

As if the strings of me had all at once 410
Gone down a tone or two; and even though
It made me scowl to think so trivial
A touch had owned the strength to tighten them,
It made me laugh to think that I was free.
But free from what—when I began to turn 415
The question round—was more than I could say:
I was no longer vexed with Killigrew,
Nor more was I possessed with Captain Craig;
But I was eased of some restraint, I thought,
Not qualified by those amenities, 420
And I should have to search the matter down;
For I was young, and I was very keen.
So I began to smoke a bad cigar
That Plunket, in his love, had given me
The night before; and as I smoked I watched 425
The flying mirrors for a mile or so,
Till to the changing glimpse, now sharp, now faint,
They gave me of the woodland over west,
A gleam of long-forgotten strenuous years
Came back, when we were Red Men on the trail, 430
With Morgan for the big chief Wocky-Bocky;
But I soon yawned out of that and set myself
To face again the loud monotonous ride
That lay before me like a vista drawn
Of bag-racks to the fabled end of things. 435

II

Yet that ride had an end, as all rides have;
And the days that followed after took the road
That all days take,—though never one of them
Went by but I got some good thought of it
For Captain Craig. Not that I pitied him, 440
Or nursed a mordant hunger for his presence;
But what I thought (what Killigrew still thinks)
An irremediable cheerfulness

Was in him and about the name of him,
And I fancy that it may be most of all   445
For the jokes he made that I have saved his letters.
I like to think of him, and how he looked—
Or should have looked—in his renewed estate,
Composing them. They may be dreariness
Unspeakable to you that never saw   450
The Captain; but to five or six of us
Who knew him they are not so bad as that.
It may be we have smiled not always where
The text itself would seem to indicate
Responsive titillation on our part,—   455
Yet having smiled at all we have done well,
For we know that we have touched the ghost of him.
He tells me that he thinks of nothing now
That he would rather do than be himself,
Wisely alive. So let us heed this man:—   460

"The world that has been old is young again,
The touch that faltered clings; and this is May.
So think of your decrepit pensioner
As one who cherishes the living light,
Forgetful of dead shadows. He may gloat,   465
And he may not have power in his arms
To make the young world move; but he has eyes
And ears, and he can read the sun. Therefore
Think first of him as one who vegetates
In tune with all the children who laugh best   470
And longest through the sunshine, though far off
Their laughter, and unheard; for 't is the child,
O friend, that with his laugh redeems the man.
Time steals the infant, but the child he leaves;
And we, we fighters over of old wars—   475
We men, we shearers of the Golden Fleece—
Were brutes without him,—brutes to tear the scars
Of one another's wounds and weep in them,

And then cry out on God that he should flaunt
For life such anguish and flesh-wretchedness.   480
But let the brute go roaring his own way:
We do not need him, and he loves us not.
Let music be for us the forward song,
And let us give the good world one more chance.

"I cannot think of anything to-day   485
That I would rather do than be myself,
Primevally alive, and have the sun
Shine into me; for on a day like this,
When the chaff-parts of a man's adversities
Are blown by quick spring breezes out of him—   490
When even a flicker of wind that wakes no more
Than a tuft of grass, or a few young yellow leaves,
Comes like the falling of a prophet's breath
On altar-flames rekindled of crushed embers,—
Then do I feel, now do I feel, within me   495
No dreariness, no grief, no discontent,
No twinge of human envy. But I beg
That you forego credentials of the past
For these illuminations of the present,
Or better still, to give the shadow justice,   500
You let me tell you something: I have yearned
In many another season for these days,
And having them with God's own pageantry
To make me glad for them,—yes, I have cursed
The sunlight and the breezes and the leaves   505
To think of men on stretchers and on beds,
Or on foul floors, like starved outrageous lizards,
Made human with paralysis and rags;
Or of some poor devil on a battle-field,
Left undiscovered and without the strength   510
To drag a maggot from his clotted mouth;
Or of women working where a man would fall—
Flat-breasted miracles of cheerfulness

Made neuter by the work that no man counts
Until it waits undone; children thrown out   515
To feed their veins and souls with offal . . . Yes,
I have had half a mind to blow my brains out
Sometimes; and I have gone from door to door,
Ragged myself, trying to do something—
Crazy, I hope.—But what has this to do   520
With Spring? Because one half of humankind
Lives here in hell, shall not the other half
Do any more than just for conscience' sake
Be miserable? Is this the way for us
To lead these creatures up to find the light,   525
Or the way to be drawn down to find the dark
Again? What is it? What does the child say?

"But let us not make riot for the child
Untaught, nor let us hold that we may read
The sun but through the shadows; nor, again,   530
Be we forgetful ever that we keep
The shadows on their side. For evidence,
I might go back a little to the days
When I had hounds and credit, and grave friends
To borrow my books and set wet glasses on them,   535
And other friends of all sorts, grave and gay,
Of whom one woman and one man stand out
From all the rest, this morning. The man said
One day, as we were riding, 'Now, you see,
There goes a woman cursed with happiness: 540
Beauty and wealth, health, horses,—everything
That she could ask, or we could ask, is hers,
Except an inward eye for the plain fact
Of what this damned world is. The cleverness
God gave her—or the devil—cautions her   545
That she must keep the china cup of life
Filled somehow, and she fills it—runs it over—
Claps her white hands while some one does the sopping

With fingers made, she thinks, for just that purpose,
Giggles and eats and reads and goes to church,   550
Makes pretty little penitential prayers,
And has an eighteen-carat crucifix
Wrapped up in chamois-skin. She gives enough,
You say; but what is giving like hers worth?
What is a gift without the soul to guide it?   555
"Poor dears, and they have cancers?—Oh!" she says;
And away she works at that new altar-cloth
For the Reverend Hieronymus Mackintosh—
Third person, Jerry. "Jerry," she says, "can say
Such lovely things, and make life seem so sweet!"   560
Jerry can drink, also.—And there she goes,
Like a whirlwind through an orchard in the springtime—
Throwing herself away as if she thought
The world and the whole planetary circus
Were a flourish of apple-blossoms. Look at her!   565
Lilies and roses! Butterflies! Great Scott!
And here is this infernal world of ours—
And hers, if only she might find it out—
Starving and shrieking, sickening, suppurating,
Whirling to God knows where . . . But look at her!   570
Confucius, how she rides! And by Saint Satan,
She's galloping over to talk with us, woman and horse
All ours! But look—just look at her!—By Jove!' . . .

"And after that it came about somehow,
Almost as if the Fates were killing time,   575
That she, the spendthrift of a thousand joys,
Rode in her turn with me, and in her turn
Made observations: 'Now there goes a man,'
She said, 'who feeds his very soul on poison:
No matter what he does, or where he looks,   580
He finds unhappiness; or, if he fails
To find it, he creates it, and then hugs it:
Pygmalion again for all the world—

Pygmalion gone wrong. You know I think
If when that precious animal was young,   585
His mother, or some watchful aunt of his,
Had spanked him with *Pendennis* and *Don Juan,*
And given him the *Lady of the Lake,*
Or *Cord and Creese,* or almost anything,
There might have been a tonic for him? Listen: 590
When he was possibly nineteen years old
He came to me and said, "I understand
You are in love"—yes, that is what he said,—
"But never mind, it won't last very long;
It never does; we all get over it.   595
We have this clinging nature, for you see
The Great Bear shook himself once on a time
And the world is one of many that let go."
But I let the creature live, and there you see him
And he would have this life no fairer thing   600
Than a certain time for numerous marionettes
To do the Dance of Death. Give him a rose,
And he will tell you it is very sweet,
But only for a day. Most wonderful!
Show him a child, or anything that laughs,   605
And he begins at once to crunch his wormwood
And then runs on with his "realities."
What does he know about realities,
Who sees the truth of things almost as well
As Nero saw the Northern Lights? Good gracious!   610
Can't you do something with him? Call him something—
Call him a type, and that will make him cry:
One of those not at all unusual,
Prophetic, would-be-Delphic manger-snappers
That always get replaced when they are gone;   615
Or one of those impenetrable men,
Who seem to carry branded on their foreheads,
"We are abstruse, but not quite so abstruse
As we think the Lord intended we should be;"

One of those men who never quite confess   620
That Washington was great;—the kind of man
That everybody knows and always will,—
Shrewd, critical, facetious, insincere,
And for the most part harmless, I'm afraid.
But even then, I truly think you ought   625
To tell him something.'—And I said I would.

"So in one afternoon you see we have
The child in absence—or, to say the least,
In ominous defect,—and in excess
Commensurate, likewise. Now the question is,   630
Not which was right and which was wrong, for each,
By virtue of one-sidedness, was both;
But rather—to my mind, as heretofore—
Is it better to be blinded by the lights,
Or by the shadows? By the lights, you say?   635
The shadows are all devils, and the lights
Gleam guiding and eternal? Very good;
But while you say so do not quite forget
That sunshine has a devil of its own,
And one that we, for the great craft of him,   640
But vaguely recognize. The marvel is
That this persuasive and especial devil,
By grace of his extreme transparency,
Precludes all common vision of him; yet
There is one way to glimpse him and a way,   645
As I believe, to test him,—granted once
That we have ousted prejudice, which means
That we have made magnanimous advance
Through self-acquaintance. Not an easy thing
For some of us; impossible, may be,   650
For all of us: the woman and the man
I cited, for example, would have wrought
The most intractable conglomerate
Of everything, if they had set themselves

To analyze themselves and not each other;   655
If only for the sake of self-respect,
They would have come to no place but the same
Wherefrom they started; one would have lived awhile
In paradise without defending it,
And one in hell without enjoying it;   660
And each had been dissuaded neither more
Nor less thereafter. There are such on earth
As might have been composed primarily
For object-lessons: he was one of them,
And she—the devil makes us hesitate: 665
'T is easy to read words writ well with ink
That makes a good black mark on smooth white paper;
But words are done sometimes with other ink
Whereof the smooth white paper gives no sign
Till science brings it out; and here we come   670
To knowledge, and the way to test a devil.

"To the greater number of us, you contend,
This demon of the sunlight is a stranger;
But if you break the sunlight of yourself,
Project it, and observe the quaint shades of it,   675
I have a shrewd suspicion you may find
That even as a name lives unrevealed
In ink that waits an agent, so it is
The devil—or this devil—hides himself
To all the diagnoses we have made   680
Save one,—sincerity. The quest is hard—
As hard as truth; but once we seem to know
That his compound obsequiousness prevails
Unferreted within us, we may find
That sympathy, which aureoles itself   685
To superfluity from you and me,
May stand against the soul for five or six
Persistent and indubitable streaks
Of irritating brilliance, out of which

A man may read, if he have knowledge in him,   690
Proportionate attest of ignorance,
Hypocrisy, good-heartedness, conceit,
Indifference,—with all of these out-hued
By the spiritual inactivity
Which more than often is identified   695
With individual intensity,
And is the parent of that selfishness
Wherof no end of lesser *tions* and *isms*
Are querulously born. But there are things
To be considered here, or your machine   700
May never justify the purchase of it;
For if you fail to gauge the difference
Between self-sacrifice and self-contempt,
Your light will be all devil and your faith
Diseased,—whatever courage you have left: 705
Courage is not enough to make men glad
For laughter when that laughter is itself
The tribute of recriminating groans;
Nor are the shapes of obsolescent creeds
Much longer to flit near enough to make   710
Men glad for living in a world like this;
But wisdom, courage, knowledge, and the faith
Which has the soul and is the soul of reason—
These are the world's achievers. And the child—
The child that is the saviour of all ages,   715
The prophet and the poet, the crown-bearer,
Must yet with Love's unhonored fortitude,
Survive to cherish and attain for us
The candor and the generosity,
By leave of which we smile if we bring back   720
Some first ideal flash that wakened us
When wisdom like a shaft of dungeon-light
Came searching down to find us.

                        "Halfway back
I made a mild allusion to the Fates,

Not knowing then that ever I should have   725
Dream-visions of them, painted on the air,—
Clotho, Lachesis, Atropos. Faint-hued
They seem, but with a faintness never fading,
Unblurred by gloom, unshattered by the sun,
Still with eternal color, colorless,   730
They move and they remain. The while I write
These very words I see them,—Atropos,
Lachesis, Clotho; and the last is laughing:
When Clotho laughs, Atropos rattles her shears;
But Clotho keeps on laughing just the same.   735
Some time when I have dreamed that Atropos
Has laughed, I'll tell you how the colors change—
The colors that are changeless, colorless."

———————

I fear I may have answered Captain Craig's
Epistle Number One with what he chose,   740
Good-humoredly but anxiously, to take
For something that was not all reverence;
From the tone of Number Two it seemed almost
As if the flanges of the old man's faith
Had slipped the treacherous rails of my allegiance,   745
And left him by the roadside, humorously
Upset, with nothing more convivial
To do than be facetious and austere:—

"If you did not like *Don César de Bazan,*
There must be some imperfection in your vitals.   750
Flamboyant and old-fashioned? Overdone?
Romantico-robustious?—Dear young man,
There are fifteen thousand ways to be one-sided,
And I have indicated two of them
Already. Now you bait me with a third—   755
As if it were a spider with nine legs;
But what it is that you would have me do,

What fatherly wrath you most anticipate,
I lack the needed impulse to discern.
If you did not like *Don César de Bazan*,   760
However, there are comedies in reach
That have the fashion always. For example:—

"At the time when there was not enough of laurel
On Parnassus to feed quite the Boston market,
An admirable poet undertook   765
With earnest fingers to graft asphodels
And old world cypress-plumes on apple-boughs;
And at the end of his experiments,
Like Johann Kepler, he brought forth a book.
The book was not sublime, but from its hard   770
And uncommutative perversity
Of words there came, like jewels out of sand,
Six measured songs too beautiful to die.
So I take that self-repudiating name
'Perversity' and throw it like a spleen   775
To the last and farthest of Thalia's kennels—
Though I who shape no songs of any sort,
I who have made no music, thrilled no canvas,—
I who have added nothing to the world
The world would reckon save long-squandered wit—   780
Might with half-pardonable reverence
Beguile my faith, maybe, to the forlorn
Extent of some sequestered murmuring
Anent the vanities. No doubt I should,
If mine were the one life that I have lived;   785
But with a few good glimpses I have had
Of heaven through the little holes in hell,
I do not any longer feel myself
To be ordained or even qualified
For criticising God to my advantage.   790
If you doubt the true humility of this,
You doubt the spectrum; and if you doubt that,

You cannot understand what price it was
The poet paid, at one time and another,
For those indemnifying sonnet-songs   795
That are to be the kernel in what lives
To shrine him when the new-born men come singing.

"Nor can you understand what I have read
From even the squeezed items of account
Which I have to my credit in that book   800
Whereof the leaves are ages and the text
Eternity. What do I care to-day
For pages that have nothing? I have lived,
And I have died, and I have lived again;
And I am very comfortable. Yes,   805
Though I look back through barren years enough
To make me seem—as I transmute myself
In a downward retrospect from what I am—
As unproductive and as unconvinced
Of the living bread and the soul's eternal draught   810
As a frog on a Passover-cake in a streamless desert,—
Still do I trust the light that I have earned,
And having earned, received. You shake your head,
But I do not know that you will shake it off.

"Meanwhile I have the flowers and the grass,   815
My brothers here the trees, and all July
To make me joyous. Why do you shake your head?
Why do you laugh?—because you are so young?
Do you think if you laugh hard enough the truth
Will go to sleep? Do you think of any couch   820
Made soft enough to put the truth to sleep?
Do you think there are no proper comedies
But yours that have the fashion? For example,
Do you think that I forget, or shall forget,
One friendless, fat, fantastic nondescript   825
Who knew the ways of laughter on low roads,—

A vagabond, a drunkard, and a sponge,
But always a free creature with a soul?
For a compliment to your intelligence
I bring him back, though not without misgivings,   830
And I caution you to damn him sparingly.

"Count Pretzel von Würzburger, the Obscene
(The beggar may have had another name,
But no man to my knowledge ever knew it)
Was a poet and a skeptic and a critic,   835
And in his own mad manner a musician:
He had found an old piano in a bar-room,
And it was his career—three nights a week,
From ten o'clock till twelve—to make it rattle;
And then, when I was just far down enough   840
To sit and watch him with his long straight hair,
And pity him, and think he looked like Liszt,
I might have glorified a musical
Steam-engine, or a xylophone. The Count
Played half of everything and 'improvised'   845
The rest: he told me once that he was born
With a genius in him that 'prohibited
Complete fidelity,' and that his art
'Confessed vagaries,' therefore. But I made
Kind reckoning of his vagaries then: 850
I had the whole great pathos of the man
To purify me, and all sorts of music
To give me spiritual nourishment
And cerebral athletics; for the Count
Played indiscriminately—with an *f*,   855
And with incurable presto—cradle-songs
And carnivals, spring-songs and funeral marches,
The Marseillaise and Schubert's Serenade—
And always in a way to make me think
Procrustes had the germ of music in him.   860
And when this interesting reprobate

Began to talk—then there were more vagaries:
He made a reeking fetich of all filth,
Apparently; but there was yet revealed
About him, through his words and on his flesh,   865
That ostracizing nimbus of a soul's
Abject, apologetic purity—
That phosphorescence of sincerity—
Which indicates the curse and the salvation
Of a life wherein starved art may never perish.   870

"One evening I remember clearliest
Of all that I passed with him. Having wrought,
With his nerve-ploughing ingenuity,
The *Träumerei* into a Titan's nightmare,
The man sat down across the table from me   875
And all at once was ominously decent.
' "The more we measure what is ours to use," '
He said then, wiping his froth-plastered mouth
With the inside of his hand, ' "the less we groan
For what the gods refuse." I've had that sleeved   880
A decade for you. Now but one more stein,
And I shall be prevailed upon to read
The only sonnet I have ever made;
And after that, if you propitiate
Gambrinus, I shall play you that Andante   885
As the world has never heard it played before.'
So saying, he produced a piece of paper,
Unfolded it, and read, 'Sonnet Unique
De Pretzel von Wurzburger, dit L'Obscéne:—

" 'Carmichael had a kind of joke-disease,   890
And he had queer things fastened on his wall.
There are three green china frogs that I recall
More potently than anything, for these
Three frogs have demonstrated, by degrees,

What curse was on the man to make him fall: 895
"They are not ordinary frogs at all,
They are the Frogs of Aristophanes."

"'God! how he laughed whenever he said that;
And how we caught from one another's eyes
The flash of what a tongue could never tell!   900
We always laughed at him, no matter what
The joke was worth. But when a man's brain dies,
We are not always glad . . . Poor Carmichael!'

"'I am a sowbug and a necrophile,'
Said Pretzel, 'and the gods are growing old;   905
The stars are singing *Golden hair to gray,*
Green leaf to yellow leaf,—or chlorophyl
To xanthophyl, to be more scientific,—
So speed me one more stein. You may believe
That I'm a mendicant, but I am not: 910
For though it look to you that I go begging,
The truth is I go giving—giving all
My strength and all my personality,
My wisdom and experience—myself,
To make it final—for your preservation;   915
Though I be not the one thing or the other,
Though I strike between the sunset and the dawn,
Though I be cliff-rubbed wreckage on the shoals
Of Circumstance,—doubt not that I comprise,
With all of my disintegrated zeal,   920
Far more than my appearance. Here he comes;
Now drink to good old Pretzel! Drink down Pretzel!
Quousque tandem, Pretzel, and O Lord,
How long! But let regret go hang: the good
Die first, and of the poor did many cease   925
To be. Beethoven after Wordsworth. *Prosit!*
There were geniuses among the trilobites,
And I suspect that I was one of them.'

"How much of him was earnest and how much
Fantastic, I know not; nor do I need   930
Profounder knowledge to exonerate
The squalor or the folly of a man
Than a consciousness—though even the crude laugh
Of indigent Priapus follow it—
That I get good of him. The poet made   935
Six golden sonnets. Well, Count Pretzel made
No golden sort of product I remember
Except a shield of wisdom for the mind
Of Captain Craig—whatever you may think
Of him or of his armor. If you like him,   940
Then some time in the future, past a doubt,
You will have him in a book, make metres of him,—
To the great delight of Mr. Killigrew,
And the grief of all your kinsmen. Christian shame
And self-confuted Orientalism   945
For the more sagacious of them; vulture-tracks
Of my Promethean bile for the rest of them;
And that will be a joke. There's nothing quite
So funny as a joke that's lost on earth
And laughed at by the gods. Your devil knows it.   950

"I come to like your Mr. Killigrew,
And I rejoice that you speak well of him.
The sprouts of human blossoming are in him,
And useful eyes—if he will open them;
But one thing ails the man. He smiles too much.   955
He comes to see me once or twice a week,
And I must tell him that he smiles too much.
If I were Socrates, how I should do it!"

———————

Epistle Number Three was longer coming.
I waited for it, even worried for it—   960
Though Killigrew, and of his own free will,

Had written reassuring little scraps
From time to time, and I had valued them
The more for being his. "The Sage," he said,
"From all that I can see, is doing well—   965
I should say very well. Three meals a day,
Siestas, and innumerable pipes—
Not to the tune of water on the stones,
But rather to the tune of his own Ego,
Which seems to be about the same as God.   970
But I was always weak in metaphysics,
And I pray therefore that you be lenient.
I'm going to be married in December,
And I have made a poem that will scan—
So Plunket says. You said the other wouldn't: 975

   "*Augustus Plunket, Ph.D.,*
     And oh, the Bishop's daughter;
   A very learned man was he
     And in twelve weeks he got her;

   And oh, she was as fair to see   980
   As pippins on the pippin tree . . .
   Tu, tui, tibi. te,—chubs in the mill water.

"Connotative, succinct, and erudite;
Three dots to boot. Now goodman Killigrew
May wind an epic one of these glad years,   985
And after that who knoweth but the Lord—
The Lord of Hosts who is the King of Glory?"

Still, when the Captain's own words were before me,
I seemed to read from them, or into them,
The protest of a mortuary joy   990
Not all substantiating Killigrew's
Off-hand assurance. The man's face came back
The while I read them, and that look again,

Which I had seen so often, came back with it.
I do not know that I can say just why,   995
But I felt the feathery touch of something wrong:—

"Since last I wrote—and I fear the weeks have gone
Too long for me to leave my gratitude
Unuttered for its own acknowledgment—
I have won, without the magic of Amphion   1000
Without the songs of Orpheus or Apollo,
The frank regard—and with it, if you like,
The fledged respect—of three quick-footed friends.
('Nothing is there more marvelous than man,'
Said Sophocles; and I say after him: 1005
'He traps and captures, all-inventive one,
The light birds and the creatures of the wold,
And in his nets the fishes of the sea.')
Once they were pictures, painted on the air,
Faint with eternal color, colorless,—   1010
But now they are not pictures, they are fowls.

"At first they stood aloof and cocked their small,
Smooth, prudent heads at me and made as if,
With a cryptic idiotic melancholy,
To look authoritative and sagacious;   1015
But when I tossed a piece of apple to them,
They scattered back with a discord of short squawks
And then came forward with a craftiness
That made me think of Eden. Atropos
Came first, and having grabbed the morsel up,   1020
Ran flapping far away and out of sight,
With Clotho and Lachesis hard after her;
But finally the three fared all alike,
And the next day I persuaded them with corn.
In a week they came and had it from my fingers   1025
And looked up at me while I pinched their bills
And made them sneeze. Count Pretzel's Carmichael

Had said they were not ordinary birds
At all,—and they are not: they are the Fates,
Foredoomed of their own insufficiency   1030
To be assimilated.—Do not think,
Because in my contented isolation
It suits me at this time to be jocose,
That I am nailing reason to the cross,
Or that I set the bauble and the bells   1035
Above the crucible; for I do nought,
Say nought, but with an ancient levity
That is the forbear of all earnestness.

"The cross, I said.—I had a dream last night:
A dream not like to any other dream   1040
That I remember. I was all alone,
Sitting as I do now beneath a tree,
But looking not, as I am looking now,
Against the sunlight. There was neither sun
Nor moon, nor do I think of any stars;   1045
Yet there was light, and there were cedar trees,
And there were sycamores. I lay at rest,
Or should have seemed at rest, within a trough
Between two giant roots. A weariness
Was on me, and I would have gone to sleep,—   1050
But I had not the courage. If I slept,
I feared that I should never wake again;
And if I did not sleep I should go mad,
And with my own dull tools, which I had used
With wretched skill so long, hack out my life.   1055
And while I lay there, tortured out of death,
Great waves of cold, as if the dead were breathing,
Came over me and through me; and I felt
Quick fearful tears of anguish on my face
And in my throat. But soon, and in the distance,   1060
Concealed, importunate, there was a sound
Of coming steps,—and I was not afraid;

No, I was not afraid then, I was glad;
For I could feel, with every thought, the Man,
The Mystery, the Child a footfall nearer.   1065
Then, when he stood before me, there was no
Surprise, there was no questioning: I knew him,
As I had known him always; and he smiled.
'Why are you here?' he asked; and reaching down,
He took up my dull blades and rubbed his thumb   1070
Across the edges of them and then smiled
Once more.—'I was a carpenter,' I said,
'But there was nothing in the world to do.'
'Nothing?' said he.—'No, nothing,' I replied.—
'But are you sure,' he asked, 'that you have skill?   1075
And are you sure that you have learned your trade?
No, you are not.'—He looked at me and laughed
As he said that; but I did not laugh then,
Although I might have laughed.—'They are dull,' said he;
'They were not very sharp if they were ground;   1080
But they are what you have, and they will earn
What you have not. So take them as they are,
Grind them and clean them, put new handles to them,
And then go learn your trade in Nazareth.
Only be sure that you find Nazareth.'—   1085
'But if I starve—what then?' said I.—He smiled.

"Now I call that as curious a dream
As ever Meleager's mother had,—
Æneas, Alcibiades, or Jacob.
I'll not except the scientist who dreamed   1090
That he was Adam and that he was Eve
At the same time; or yet that other man
Who dreamed that he was Æschylus, reborn
To clutch, combine, compensate, and adjust
The plunging and unfathomable chorus   1095
Wherein we catch, like a bacchanale through thunder,
The chanting of the new Eumenides,

Implacable, renascent, farcical,
Triumphant, and American. He did it,
But he did it in a dream. When he awoke   1100
One phrase of it remained; one verse of it
Went singing through the remnant of his life
Like a bag-pipe through a mad-house.—He died young,
And the more I ponder the small history
That I have gleaned of him by scattered roads,   1105
The more do I rejoice that he died young.
That measure would have chased him all his days,
Defeated him, deposed him, wasted him,
And shrewdly ruined him—though in that ruin
There would have lived, as always it has lived, 1110
In ruin as in failure, the supreme
Fulfilment unexpressed, the rhythm of God
That beats unheard through songs of shattered men
Who dream but cannot sound it.—He declined,
From all that I have ever learned of him,   1115
With absolute good-humor. No complaint,
No groaning at the burden which is light,
No brain-waste of impatience—'Never mind,'
He whispered, 'for I might have written Odes.'

"Speaking of odes now makes me think of ballads. 1120
Your admirable Mr. Killigrew
Has latterly committed what he calls
A Ballad of London—London 'Town,' of course—
And he has wished that I pass judgment on it.
He says there is a 'generosity'   1125
About it, and a 'sympathetic insight;'
And there are strong lines in it, so he says.
But who am I that he should make of me
A judge? You are his friend, and you know best
The measure of his jingle. I am old,   1130
And you are young. Be sure, I may go back
To squeak for you the tunes of yesterday

On my old fiddle—or what's left of it—
And give you as I'm able a young sound;
But all the while I do it I remain   1135
One of Apollo's pensioners (and yours),
An usher in the Palace of the Sun,
A candidate for mattocks and trombones
(The brass-band will be indispensable),
A patron of high science, but no critic.   1140
So I shall have to tell him, I suppose,
That I read nothing now but Wordsworth, Pope,
Lucretius, Robert Burns, and William Shakespeare.
Now this is Mr. Killigrew's performance:

> " '*Say, do you go to London Town,*   1145
> *You with the golden feather?'*—
> '*And if I go to London Town*
> *With my golden feather?'*—
> '*These autumn roads are bright and brown,*
> *The season wears a russet crown;*   1150
> *And if you go to London Town,*
> *We'll go down together.'*

"I cannot say for certain, but I think
The brown bright nightingale was half assuaged
Before your Mr. Killigrew was born.   1155
If I have erred in my chronology,
No matter,—for the feathered man sings now:

> " '*Yes, I go to London Town'*
> (*Merrily waved the feather*),
> '*And if you go to London Town,*   1160
> *Yes, we'll go together.'*
> *So in the autumn bright and brown,*
> *Just as the year began to frown,*
> *All the way to London Town*
> *Rode the two together.*   1165

" '*I go to marry a fair maid*'
  (*Lightly swung the feather*)—
'*Pardie, a true and loyal maid*'
  (*Oh, the swinging feather!*)—
'*For us the wedding gold is weighed,*   1170
For us the feast will soon be laid;
We'll make a gallant show,' *he said,*—
  '*She and I together.*'

"The feathered man will do a thousand things
And the world go smiling; but the feathered man   1175
May do too much. Now mark how he continues:

" '*And you—you go to London Town?*'
  (*Breezes waved the feather*)—
'*Yes, I go to London Town.*'
  (*Ah, the stinging feather!*)—   1180
'*Why do you go, my merry blade?*
Like me, to marry a fair maid?'—
'*Why do I go? . . . God knows,*' *he said;*
  And on they rode together.

"Now you have read it through, and you know best   1185
What worth it has. We fellows with gray hair
Who march with sticks to music that is gray
Judge not your vanguard fifing. You are one
To judge; and you will tell me what you think:—
Barring the Town, the Fair Maid, and the Feather,   1190
The dialogue and those parentheses,
You cherish it, undoubtedly. Pardee!
You call it, with a few conservative
Allowances, an excellent small thing
For patient inexperience to do: 1195
Derivative, you say,—still rather pretty.
But what is wrong with Mr. Killigrew?

Is he in love, or has he read Rossetti?—
Forgive me! I am old and doddering . . .
When are you coming back to Tilbury Town?"   1200

I could forgive the Captain soon enough,
But Killigrew—there was a question there;
Nor was it answered when the next week brought
A letter from him. After rocketing
For six or seven pages about love,   1205
Truth, purity, the passion of the soul,
And other salutary attributes,
Discovered or miraculously born
Within six months, he said: "The Patriarch
Is not quite as he should be. There's a clutch   1210
Of something on him that will not let go;
And there are days together when his eyes
Are like two lamps in ashes. The gray look,
Which we thought once the glory and the crown
Of your too flexible determinist,   1215
Has gone all over him. And when he laughs,
He waits as if to hear the angels weep:
It seems to make him sorry when he laughs,
And I know what it does to me. But here
As at the station—I remember that—   1220
The quantitative bias of the boy
May slant me too much to the other side
And make me blind again. By Jove! old man,
If you could really know her as I do
'Twould be the revelation of your life: 1225
You would see that there are women in the world
Who are altogether different," etc.

There was more generosity in "women"
I thought than in the man without the feather.—
Meanwhile I saw that Captain Craig was dying.   1230

III

I found the old man sitting in his bed,
Propped up and uncomplaining. On a chair
Beside him was a dreary bowl of broth,
A magazine, some glasses, and a pipe.
"I do not light it nowadays," he said,   1235
"But keep it for an antique influence
That it exerts, an aura that it sheds—
Like hautboys, or Provence. You understand:
The charred memorial defeats us yet,
But think you not for always. We are young,   1240
And we are friends of time. Time that made smoke
Will drive away the smoke, and we shall know
The work that we are doing. We shall build
With embers of all shrines one pyramid,
And we shall have the most resplendent flame   1245
From earth to heaven, as the old words go,
And we shall need no smoke . . . Why don't you laugh?"

I gazed into those calm, half-lighted eyes
And smiled at them with grim obedience.
He told me that I did it very well,   1250
But added that I should undoubtedly
Do better in the future: "There is nothing,"
He said, "so beneficial in a sick-room
As a well-bred spontaneity of manner.
Your sympathetic scowl obtrudes itself,   1255
And is indeed surprising. After death,
Were you to take it with you to your coffin
An unimaginative man might think
That you had lost your life in worrying
To find out what it was that worried you.   1260
The ways of unimaginative men
Are singularly fierce . . . Why do you stand?
Sit here and watch me while I take this soup.
The doctor likes it, therefore it is good.

"The man who wrote the decalogue," pursued   1265
The Captain, having swallowed four or five
Heroic spoonfuls of his lukewarm broth,
"Forgot the doctors. And I think sometimes
The man of Galilee (or, if you choose,
The men who made the sayings of the man)   1270
Like Buddha, and the others who have seen,
Was to men's loss the Poet—though it be
The Poet only of him we revere,
The Poet we remember. We have put
The prose of him so far away from us,   1275
The fear of him so crudely over us,
That I have wondered—wondered."—Cautiously,
But yet as one were cautious in a dream,
He set the bowl down on the chair again,
Crossed his thin fingers, looked me in the face,   1280
And looking smiled a little. "Go away,"
He said at last, "and let me go to sleep.
I told you I should eat, but I shall not.
To-morrow I shall eat; and I shall read
Some clauses of a jocund instrument   1285
That I have been preparing here of late
For you and for the rest, assuredly.
'Attend the testament of Captain Craig:
Good citizens, good fathers and your sons,
Good mothers and your daughters.' I should say so.   1290
Now go away and let me go to sleep."

I stood before him and held out my hand,
He took it, pressed it; and I felt again
The sick soft closing on it. He would not
Let go, but lay there, looking up to me   1295
With eyes that had a sheen of water on them
And a faint wet spark within them. So he clung,
Tenaciously, with fingers icy warm,
And eyes too full to keep the sheen unbroken.

I looked at him. The fingers closed hard once,   1300
And then fell down.—I should have left him then.

But when we found him the next afternoon,
My first thought was that he had made his eyes
Miraculously smaller. They were sharp
And hard and dry, and the spark in them was dry.   1305
For a glance it all but seemed as if the man
Had artfully forsworn the brimming gaze
Of yesterday, and with a wizard strength
Inveigled in, reduced, and vitalized
The straw-shine of October; and had that   1310
Been truth, we should have humored him not less,
Albeit he had fooled us,—for he said
That we had made him glad by coming to him.
And he was glad: the manner of his words
Revealed the source of them; and the gray smile   1315
Which lingered like a twilight on his face
Told of its own slow fading that it held
The promise of the sun. Cadaverous,
God knows it was; and we knew it was honest.

"So you have come to have the old man read   1320
To you from his last will and testament:
Well, it will not be long—not very long—
So listen." He brought out from underneath
His pillow a new manuscript, and said,
"You are doing well to come and have me read   1325
My testament. There are men in the world
Who say of me, if they remember me,
That I am poor;—and I believe the ways
Of certain men who never find things out
Are stranger than the way Lord Bacon wrote   1330
Leviticus, and *Faust.*" He fixed his eyes
Abstractedly on something far from us,
And with a look that I remembered well

Gazed hard the while we waited. But at length
He found himself and soon began to chant,   1335
With a fitful shift at thin sonorousness
The jocund instrument; and had he been
Definitively parceling to us
All Kimberley and half of Ballarat,
The lordly quaver of his poor old words   1340
Could not have been the more magniloquent.
No promise of dead carbon or of gold,
However, flashed in ambush to corrupt us:

"I, Captain Craig, abhorred iconoclast,
Sage-errant, favored of the Cosmic Joke,   1345
And self-reputed humorist at large,
Do now, confessed of my world-worshiping,
Time-questioning, sun-fearing, and heart-yielding,
Approve and unreservedly devise
To you and your assigns for evermore,   1350
God's universe and yours. If I had won
What first I sought, I might have made you beam
By giving less; but now I make you laugh
By giving more than what had made you beam,
And it is well. No man has ever done   1355
The deed of humor that God promises,
But now and then we know tragedians
Reform, and in denial too divine
For sacrifice, too firm for ecstasy,
Record in jolly letters or in books   1360
What fragment of God's laughter they have caught,
What earnest of its rhythm; and I believe
That I, in having somewhat recognized
The formal measure of it, have endured
The discord of infirmity not less   1365
Through fortune than by failure. What men lose,
Man gains; and what man gains reports itself

In losses we but vaguely deprecate,
So they be not for us;—and this is right,
Except that when the devil in the sun   1370
Misguides us we go darkly where the shine
Misleads us, and we know not what we see:
We know not if we climb or if we fall;
And if we fly, we know not where we fly.

"And here do I insert an urging clause   1375
For climbers and up-fliers of all sorts,
Cliff-climbers and high-fliers: Phaethon,
Bellerophon, and Icarus did each
Go gloriously up, and each in turn
Did famously come down—as you have read   1380
In poems and elsewhere; but other men
Have mounted where no fame has followed them,
And we have had no sight, no news of them,
And we have heard no crash. The crash may count,
Undoubtedly, and earth be fairer for it;   1385
Yet none save creatures out of harmony
Have ever, in their fealty to the flesh,
Made crashing an ideal. It is the flesh
That ails us, for the spirit knows no qualm,
No failure, no down-falling: so climb high,   1390
And having set your steps regard not much
The downward laughter clinging at your feet,
Nor overmuch the warning; only know,
As well as you know dawn from lantern-light,
That far above you, for you, and within you,   1395
There burns and shines and lives, unwavering
And always yours, the truth. Take on yourself
But your sincerity, and you take on
Good promise for all climbing: fly for truth,
And hell shall have no storm to crush your flight,   1400
No laughter to vex down your loyalty.

"I think you may be smiling at me now—
And if I make you smile, so much the better;
For I would have you know that I rejoice
Always to see the thing that I would see—   1405
The righteous thing, the wise thing. I rejoice
Always to think that any thought of mine,
Or any word or any deed of mine,
May grant sufficient of what fortifies
Good feeling and the courage of calm joy   1410
To make the joke worth while. Contrariwise,
When I review some faces I have known—
Sad faces, hungry faces—and reflect
On thoughts I might have moulded, human words
I might have said, straightway it saddens me   1415
To feel perforce that had I not been mute
And actionless, I might have made them bright
Somehow, though only for the moment. Yes,
Howbeit I confess the vanities,
It saddens me;—and sadness, of all things   1420
Miscounted wisdom, and the most of all
When warmed with old illusions and regrets,
I mark the selfishest, and on like lines
The shrewdest. For your sadness makes you climb
With dragging footsteps, and it makes you groan;   1425
It hinders you when most you would be free,
And there are many days it wearies you
Beyond the toil itself. And if the load
It lays on you may not be shaken off
Till you have known what now you do not know—   1430
Meanwhile you climb; and he climbs best who sees
Above him truth burn faithfulest, and feels
Within him truth burn purest. Climb or fall,
One road remains and one firm guidance always;
One way that shall be taken, climb or fall.   1435

"But 'falling, falling, falling.' There's your song,
The cradle-song that sings you to the grave.
What is it your bewildered poet says?—

   " *'The toiling ocean thunders of unrest*
     And aching desolation; the still sea   1440
     Paints but an outward calm that mocks itself
     To the final and irrefragable sleep
     That owns no shifting fury; and the shoals
     Of ages are but records of regret
     Where Time, the sun's arch-phantom, writes on sand   1445
     The prelude of his ancient nothingness.'

   " 'T is easy to compound a dirge like that,
And it is easy too to be deceived
And alienated by the fleshless note
Of half-world yearning in it; but the truth   1450
To which we all are tending,—charlatans
And architects alike, artificers
In tinsel as in gold, evangelists
Of ruin and redemption, all alike,—
The truth we seek and equally the truth   1455
We do not seek, but yet may not escape,
Was never found alone through flesh contempt
Or through flesh reverence. Look east and west
And we may read the story: where the light
Shone first the shade now darkens; where the shade   1460
Clung first, the light fights westward—though the shade
Still feeds, and there is yet the Orient.

"But there is this to be remembered always:
Whatever be the altitude you reach,
You do not rise alone; nor do you fall   1465
But you drag others down to more or less
Than your preferred abasement. God forbid

That ever I should preach, and in my zeal
Forget that I was born an humorist;
But now, for once, before I go away,   1470
I beg of you to be magnanimous
A moment, while I speak to please myself—
The moment now for flowers; and your patience:

"Though I have heard it variously sung
That even in the fury and the clash   1475
Of battles, and the closer fights of men
When silence gives the knowing world no sign,
One flower there is, though crushed and cursed it be,
Keeps rooted through all tumult and all scorn,—
Still do I find, when I look sharply down,   1480
There's yet another flower that grows well
And has the most unconscionable roots
Of any weed on earth. Perennial
It grows, and has the name of Selfishness;
No doubt you call it Love. In either case,   1485
You propagate it with a diligence
That hardly were outmeasured had its leaf
The very juice in it of that famed herb
Which gave back breath to Glaucus; and I know
That in the twilight, after the day's work,   1490
You take your little children in your arms,
Or lead them by their credulous frail hands
Benignly out and through the garden-gate
And show them there the things that you have raised;
Not everything, perchance, but always one   1495
Miraculously rooted flower plot
Which is your pride, their pattern. Socrates,
Could he be with you there at such a time,
Would have some unsolicited shrewd words
To say that you might hearken to; but I   1500
Say nothing, for I am not Socrates.—
So much, good friends, for flowers; and I thank you.

"There was a poet once who would have roared
Away the world and had an end of stars.
Where was he when I quoted him?—oh, yes: 1505
'T is easy for a man to link loud words
With woeful pomp and unschooled emphasis
And add one thundered contribution more
To the dirges of all-hollowness, I said;
But here again I find the question set   1510
Before me, after turning books on books
And looking soulward through man after man,
If there indeed be more determining
Play-service in remotely sounding down
The world's one-sidedness. If I judge right,   1515
Your pounding protestations, echoing
Their burden of unfraught futility,
Surge back to mute forgetfulness at last
And have a kind of sunny, sullen end,
Like any cold north storm.—But there are few   1520
Still seas that have no life to profit them,
And even in such currents of the mind
As have no tide-rush to them, but are drowsed,
Crude thoughts may dart in armor and upspring
With a waking sound, when all is dim with peace,   1525
Like sturgeons in the twilight out of Lethe;
And though they be discordant, hard, grotesque,
And all unwelcome to the lethargy
That you think means repose, you know as well
As if your names were shouted when they leap,   1530
And when they leap you listen.—Ah! friends, friends,
There are these things we do not like to know:
They trouble us, they make us hesitate,
They touch us, and we try to put them off.
We banish one another and then say   1535
That we are left alone: the midnight leaf
That rattles when it hangs above the snow—
Gaunt, fluttering, forlorn—scarcely may seem

So cold in all its palsied loneliness
As we, we frozen brothers, who have yet   1540
Profoundly and severely to find out
That there is more of unpermitted love
In most men's reticence than most men think.

"Once, when I made it out fond-headedness
To say that we should ever be apprised   1545
Of our deserts and their emolument
At all but in the specious way of words,
The wisdom of a warm thought woke within me
And I could read the sun. Then did I turn
My long-defeated face full to the world,   1550
And through the clouded warfare of it all
Discern the light. Through dusk that hindered it,
I found the truth, and for the first whole time
Knew then that we were climbing. Not as one
Who mounts along with his experience   1555
Bound on him like an Old Man of the Sea—
Not as a moral pedant who drags chains
Of his unearned ideals after him
And always to the lead-like thud they make
Attunes a cold inhospitable chant   1560
Of All Things Easy to the Non-Attached,—
But as a man, a scarred man among men,
I knew it, and I felt the strings of thought
Between us to pull tight the while I strove;
And if a curse came ringing now and then   1565
To my defended ears, how could I know
The light that burned above me and within me,
And at the same time put on cap-and-bells
For such as yet were groping?"

                          Killigrew
Made there as if to stifle a small cough.   1570
I might have kicked him, but regret forbade

The subtle admonition; and indeed
When afterwards I reprimanded him,
The fellow never knew quite what I meant.
I may have been unjust.—The Captain read   1575
Right on, without a chuckle or a pause,
As if he had heard nothing:

                                    "How, forsooth,
Shall any man, by curses or by groans,
Or by the laugh-jarred stillness of all hell,
Be so drawn down to servitude again   1580
That on some backward level of lost laws
And undivined relations, he may know
No longer Love's imperative resource,
Firm once and his, well treasured then, but now
Too fondly thrown away? And if there come   1585
But once on all his journey, singing down
To find him, the gold-throated forward call,
What way but one, what but the forward way,
Shall after that call guide him? When his ears
Have earned an inward skill to methodize   1590
The clash of all crossed voices and all noises,
How shall he grope to be confused again,
As he has been, by discord? When his eyes
Have read the book of wisdom in the sun,
And after dark deciphered it on earth,   1595
How shall he turn them back to scan some huge
Blood-lettered protest of bewildered men
That hunger while he feeds where they should starve
And all absurdly perish?"

                        Killigrew
Looked hard for a subtile object on the wall,   1600
And, having found it, sighed. The Captain paused:
If he grew tedious, most assuredly
Did he crave pardon of us; he had feared

Beforehand that he might be wearisome,
But there was not much more of it, he said,— 1605
No more than just enough. And we rejoiced
That he should look so kindly on us then.
("Commend me to a dying man's grimace
For absolute humor, always," Killigrew
Maintains; but I know better.)

                        "Work for them, 1610
You tell me? Work the folly out of them?
Go back to them and teach them how to climb,
While you teach caterpillars how to fly?
You tell me that Alnaschar is a fool
Because he dreams? And what is this you ask? 1615
I make him wise? I teach him to be still?
While you go polishing the Pyramids,
I hold Alnaschar's feet? And while you have
The ghost of Memnon's image all day singing,
I sit with aching arms and hardly catch 1620
A few spilled echoes of the song of songs—
The song that I should have as utterly
For mine as any other man should have,
The sweetest a glad shepherd ever trilled
In Sharon, long ago? Is this the way 1625
For me to do good climbing any more
Than Phaethon's? Do you think the golden tone
Of that far-singing call you all have heard
Means any more for you than you should be
Wise-heartedly, glad-heartedly yourselves? 1630
Do this, there is no more for you to do;
And you have no dread left, no shame, no scorn.
And while you have your wisdom and your gold,
Songs calling, and the Princess in your arms,
Remember, if you like, from time to time, 1635
Down yonder where the clouded millions go,

Your bloody-knuckled scullions are not slaves,
Your children of Alnaschar are not fools.

"Nor are they quite so foreign or far down
As you may think to see them. What you take   1640
To be the cursedest mean thing that crawls
On earth is nearer to you than you know:
You may not ever crush him but you lose,
You may not ever shield him but you gain—
As he, with all his crookedness, gains with you.   1645
Your preaching and your teaching, your achieving,
Your lifting up and your discovering,
Are more than often—more than you have dreamed—
The world-refracted evidence of what
Your dream denies. You cannot hide yourselves   1650
In any multitude or solitude,
Or mask yourselves in any studied guise
Of hardness or of old humility,
But soon by some discriminating man—
Some humorist at large, like Socrates—   1655
You get yourselves found out.—Now I should be
Found out without an effort. For example:
When I go riding, trimmed and shaved again,
Consistent, adequate, respectable,—
Some citizen, for curiosity,   1660
Will ask of a good neighbor, 'What is this?'—
'It is the funeral of Captain Craig,'
Will be the neighbor's word.—'And who, good man,
Was Captain Craig?'—'He was an humorist;
And we are told that there is nothing more   1665
For any man alive to say of him.'—
'There is nothing very strange in that,' says A;
'But the brass band? What has he done to be
Blown through like this by cornets and trombones?
And here you have this incompatible dirge—   1670
Where are the jokes in that?'—Then B should say:

'Maintained his humor: nothing more or less.
The story goes that on the day before
He died—some say a week, but that's a trifle—
He said, with a subdued facetiousness,   1675
"Play Handel, not Chopin; assuredly not
Chopin." '—He was indeed an humorist."

He made the paper fall down at arm's length;
And with a tension of half-quizzical
Benignity that made it hard for us,   1680
He looked up—first at Morgan, then at me—
Almost, I thought, as if his eyes would ask
If we were satisfied; and as he looked,
The tremor of an old heart's weariness
Was on his mouth. He gazed at each of us,   1685
But spoke no further word that afternoon.
He put away the paper, closed his eyes,
And went to sleep with his lips flickering;
And after that we left him.—At midnight
Plunket and I looked in; but he still slept,   1690
And everything was going as it should.
The watchman yawned, rattled his newspaper,
And wondered what it was that ailed his lamp.
He said it wheezed. He feared it might explode.

Next day we found the Captain wide awake,   1695
Propped up, and searching dimly with a spoon
Through another dreary dish of chicken-broth,
Which he raised up to me, at my approach,
So fervently and so unconsciously,
That one could only laugh. He looked again   1700
At each of us, and as he looked he frowned;
And there was something in that frown of his
That none of us had ever seen before.
"Kind friends," he said, "be sure that I rejoice
To know that you have come to visit me;   1705

Be sure I speak with undisguised words
And earnest, when I say that I rejoice."—
"But what the devil!" whispered Killigrew.
I kicked him, for I thought I understood.

The old man's eyes had glimmered wearily   1710
At first, but now they glittered like to those
Of a glad fish. "Beyond a doubt," said he,
"My dream this morning was more singular
Than any other I have ever known.
Give me that I might live ten thousand years,   1715
And all those years do nothing but have dreams,
I doubt me much if any one of them
Could be so quaint or so fantastical,
So pregnant, as a dream of mine this morning.
You may not think it any more than odd;   1720
You may not feel—you cannot wholly feel—
How droll it was:—I dreamed that I found Hamlet—
Found him at work, drenched with an angry sweat,
Predestined, he declared with emphasis,
To root out a large weed on Lethe wharf;   1725
And after I had watched him for some time,
I laughed at him and told him that no root
Would ever come the while he talked like that:
The power was not in him, I explained,
For such compound accomplishment. He glared   1730
At me, of course,—next moment laughed at me,
And finally laughed with me. I was right,
And we had eisel on the strength of it:—
'They tell me that this water is not good,'
Said Hamlet, and you should have seen him smile.   1735
Conceited? Pelion on Ossa? pah! . . .

"But anon comes in a crocodile. We stepped
Adroitly down upon the back of him,
And away we went to an undiscovered country—

A fertile place, but in more ways than one   1740
So like the region we had started from,
That Hamlet straightway found another weed
And there began to tug. I laughed again,
Till he cried out on me and on my mirth,
Protesting all he knew: 'The Fates,' he said,   1745
'Have ordered it that I shall have these roots.'
But all at once a dreadful hunger seized him,
And it was then we killed the crocodile—
Killed him and ate him. Washed with eisel down
That luckless reptile was, to the last morsel;   1750
And there we were with flag-fens all around us,—
And there was Hamlet, at his task again,
Ridiculous. And while I watched him work,
The drollest of all changes came to pass:—
The weed had snapped off just above the root,   1755
Not warning him, and I was left alone.
The bubbles rose, and I laughed heartily
To think of him; I laughed when I woke up;
And when my soup came in I laughed again;
I think I may have laughed a little—no?—   1760
Not when you came? . . . Why do you look like that?
You don't believe me? Crocodiles—why not?
Who knows what he has eaten in his life?
Who knows but I have eaten Atropos? . . .
'Briar and oak for a soldier's crown,' you say?   1765
Provence? Oh, no . . . Had I been Socrates,
Count Pretzel would have been the King of Spain."

Now of all casual things we might have said
To make the matter smooth at such a time,
There may have been a few that we had found   1770
Sufficient. Recollection fails, however,
To say that we said anything. We looked.
Had he been Carmichael, we might have stood
Like faithful hypocrites and laughed at him;

But the Captain was not Carmichael at all,   1775
For the Captain had no frogs: he had the sun.
So there we waited, hungry for the word,—
Tormented, unsophisticated, stretched—
Till, with a drawl, to save us, Killigrew
Good-humoredly spoke out. The Captain fixed   1780
His eyes on him with some severity.

"That was a funny dream, beyond a doubt,"
Said Killigrew;—"too funny to be laughed at;
Too humorous, we mean."—"Too humorous?"
The Captain answered; "I approve of that.   1785
Proceed."—We were not glad for Killigrew.

"Well," he went on, " 't was only this. You see
My dream this morning was a droll one too:
I dreamed that a sad man was in my room,
Sitting, as I do now, beside the bed.   1790
I questioned him, but he made no reply,—
Said not a word, but sang."—"Said not a word,
But sang," the Captain echoed. "Very good.
Now tell me what it was the sad man sang."
"Now that," said Killigrew, constrainedly,   1795
And with a laugh that might have been left out,
"Is why I know it must have been a dream.
But there he was, and I lay in the bed
Like you; and I could see him just as well
As you see my right hand. And for the songs   1800
He sang to me—there's where the dream part comes."

"You don't remember them?" the Captain said,
With a weary little chuckle; "very well,
I might have guessed it. Never mind your dream,
But let me go to sleep."—For a moment then   1805
There was half a frown on Killigrew's good face,
But he turned it to a smile.—"Not quite," said he;

"The songs that he sang first were sorrowful,
And they were stranger than the man himself—
And he was very strange; but I found out,   1810
Through all the gloom of him and of his music,
That a kind of—well, say mystic cheerfulness,
Or give it almost any trumped-up name,
Pervaded him; for slowly, as he sang,
There came a change, and I began to know   1815
The method of it all. Song after song
Was ended; and when I had listened there
For hours—I mean for dream-hours—hearing him,
And always glad that I was hearing him,
There came another change—a great one. Tears   1820
Rolled out at last like bullets from his eyes,
And I could hear them fall down on the floor
Like shoes; and they were always marking time
For the song that he was singing. I have lost
The greater number of his verses now,   1825
But there are some, like these, that I remember:

> " 'Ten men from Zanzibar,
> Black as iron hammers are,
> Riding on a cable-car
> Down to Crowley's theater.' . . .   1830

"Ten men?" the Captain interrupted there—
"Ten men, my Euthyphron? That is beautiful.
But never mind, I wish to go to sleep:
Tell Cebes that I wish to go to sleep. . . .
O ye of little faith, your golden plumes   1835
Are like to drag . . . par-dee!"—We may have smiled
In after days to think how Killigrew
Had sacrificed himself to fight that silence,
But we were grateful to him, none the less;
And if we smiled, that may have been the reason.   1840
But the good Captain for a long time then

Said nothing: he lay quiet—fast asleep,
For all that we could see. We waited there
Till each of us, I fancy, must have made
The paper on the wall begin to squirm,   1845
And then got up to leave. My friends went out,
And I was going, when the old man cried:
"You leave me now—now it has come to this?
What have I done to make you go? Come back!
Come back!"

        There was a quaver in his cry   1850
That we shall not forget—reproachful, kind,
Indignant, piteous. It seemed as one
Marooned on treacherous tide-feeding sand
Were darkly calling over the still straits
Between him and irrevocable shores   1855
Where now there was no lamp to fade for him,
No call to give him answer. We were there
Before him, but his eyes were not much turned
On us; nor was it very much to us
That he began to speak the broken words,   1860
The scattered words, that he had left in him.

"So it has come to this? And what is this?
Death, do you call it? Death? And what is death?
Why do you look like that at me again?
Why do you shrink your brows and shut your lips?   1865
If it be fear, then I can do no more
Than hope for all of you that you may find
Your promise of the sun; if it be grief
You feel, to think that this old face of mine
May never look at you and laugh again,   1870
Then tell me why it is that you have gone
So long with me, and followed me so far,
And had me to believe you took my words
For more than ever misers did their gold?"

He listened, but his eyes were far from us—   1875
Too far to make us turn to Killigrew,
Or search the futile shelves of our own thoughts
For golden-labeled insincerities
To make placebos of. The marrowy sense
Of a slow November storm that splashed against   1880
The shingles and the glass reminded us
That we had brought umbrellas. He continued:

"Oh, can it be that I, too credulous,
Have made myself believe that you believe
Yourselves to be the men that you are not?   1885
I prove and I prize well your friendliness,
But I would have that your last look at me
Be not like this; for I would scan to-day
Strong thoughts on all your faces—no regret,
No fine commiseration—oh, not that,   1890
Not that! Nor say of me, when I am gone,
That I was cold and harsh, for I was warm
To strangeness, and for you . . . Say not like that
Of me—nor think of me that I reproached
The friends of my tight battles and hard years,   1895
But say that I did love them to the last
And in my love reproved them for the grief
They did not—for they dared not—throw away.
Courage, my boys,—courage, is what you need:
Courage that is not all flesh-recklessness,   1900
But earnest of the world and of the soul—
First of the soul; for a man may be as brave
As Ajax in the fury of his arms,
And in the midmost warfare of his thoughts
Be frail as Paris . . . For the love, therefore,   1905
That brothered us when we stood back that day
From Delium—the love that holds us now
More than it held us at Amphipolis—
Forget you not that he who in his work

Would mount from these low roads of measured shame   1910
To tread the leagueless highway must fling first
And fling forevermore beyond his reach
The shackles of a slave who doubts the sun.
There is no servitude so fraudulent
As of a sun-shut mind; for 't is the mind   1915
That makes you craven or invincible,
Diseased or puissant. The mind will pay
Ten thousand fold and be the richer then
To grant new service; but the world pays hard,
And accurately sickens till in years   1920
The dole has eked its end and there is left
What all of you are noting on all days
In these Athenian streets, where squandered men
Drag ruins of half-warriors to the grave—
Or to Hippocrates."

             His head fell back,   1925
And he lay still with wearied eyes half-closed.
We waited, but a few faint words yet stayed:
"Kind friends," he said, "friends I have known so long,
Though I have jested with you in time past,
Though I have stung your pride with epithets   1930
Not all forbearing,—still, when I am gone,
Say Socrates wrought always for the best
And for the wisest end . . . Give me the cup!
The truth is yours, God's universe is yours . . .
Good-by . . . good citizens . . . give me the cup" . . .   1935
Again we waited; and this time we knew
Those lips of his that would not flicker down
Had yet some fettered message for us there.
We waited, and we watched him. All at once,
With a faint flash, the clouded eyes grew clear,   1940
And then we knew the man was coming back,
And we knew that he would speak in the old way.
We watched him, and I listened. The man smiled

And looked about him—not regretfully,
Not anxiously; and when at last he spoke,   1945
Before the long drowse came to give him peace,
One word was all he said. "Trombones," he said.

That evening, at "The Chrysalis" again,
We smoked and looked at one another's eyes,
And we were glad. The world had scattered ways   1950
For us to take, we knew; but for the time
That one snug room where big beech logs roared smooth
Defiance to the cold rough rain outside
Sufficed. There were no scattered ways for us
That we could see just then, and we were glad: 1955
We were glad to be on earth, and we rejoiced
No less for Captain Craig that he was gone.
We might, for his dead benefit, have run
The gamut of all human weaknesses
And uttered after-platitudes enough—   1960
Wrecked on his own abstractions, and all such—
To drive away Gambrinus and the bead
From Bernard's ale; and I suppose we might
Have praised, accordingly, the Lord of Hosts
For making us to see that we were not   1965
(Like certain unapproved inferiors
Whom we had known, and having known might name)
Abominable flotsam. But the best
And wisest occupation, we had learned,—
At work, at home, or at "The Chrysalis,"   1970
Companioned or unfriended, winged or chained,—
Was always to perpetuate the bead.

So Plunket, who had knowledge of all sorts,
Yet hardly ever spoke, began to plink
O tu, Palermo!—quaintly, with his nails,—   1975
On Morgan's fiddle, and at once got seized,

As if he were some small thing, by the neck.
Then the consummate Morgan, having told
Explicitly what hardship might accrue
To Plunket if he did that any more,   1980
Made roaring chords and acrobatic runs—
To charge his fingers and the strings, he said,—
And then, with his kind eyes on Killigrew,
Struck up the schoolgirls' march in *Lohengrin*,
So Killigrew might smile and stretch himself   1985
And have to light his pipe. When that was done
We knew that Morgan, by the looks of him,
Was in the mood for almost anything
From Bach to Offenbach;—and of all times
That he has ever played, that one somehow—   1990
That evening of the day the Captain died—
Stands out like one great verse of a good song,
One strain that sings itself beyond the rest
For the magic and a glamour that it has.

The ways have scattered for us, and all things   1995
Have changed; and we have wisdom, I doubt not,
More fit for the world's work than we had then;
But neither parted roads nor cent per cent
May starve quite out the child that lives in us—
The Child that is the Man, the Mystery,   2000
The Phœnix of the World. So, now and then,
That evening of the day the Captain died
Returns to us; and there comes always with it
The storm, the warm restraint, the fellowship,
The friendship and the firelight, and the fiddle.   2005
So too there comes a day that followed it—
A windy, dreary day with a cold white shine
That only gummed the tumbled frozen ruts
We tramped upon. The road was hard and long,
But we had what we knew to comfort us,   2010
And we had the large humor of the thing

To make it advantageous; for men stopped
And eyed us on that road from time to time,
And on that road the children followed us;
And all along that road the Tilbury Band   2015
Blared indiscreetly the Dead March in Saul.

ISAAC AND ARCHIBALD

Isaac and Archibald were two old men.
I knew them, and I may have laughed at them
A little; but I must have honored them
For they were old, and they were geniuses.

I do not think of either of them now   5
Without remembering, infallibly,
A journey that I made one afternoon
With Isaac to find out what Archibald
Was doing with his oats. It was high time
Those oats were cut, said Isaac; and he feared   10
That Archibald—well, he could never feel
Quite sure of Archibald. Accordingly
The good old man invited me—that is,
Permitted me—to go along with him;
And I, with a small boy's adhesiveness   15
To competent old age, got up and went.
I do not know that I cared overmuch
For Archibald's or anybody's oats,
But Archibald was quite another thing,
And Isaac yet another; and the world   20
Was wide, and there was gladness everywhere.
We walked together down the River Road
With all the warmth and wonder of the land
Around us, and the wayside flash of leaves,—
And Isaac said the day was glorious;   25

But somewhere at the end of the first mile
I found that I was figuring to find
How long those ancient legs of his would keep
The pace that he had set for them. The sun
Was hot, and I was ready to sweat blood;   30
But Isaac, for aught I could make of him,
Was cool to his hat-band. So I said then
With a dry gasp of affable despair,
Something about the scorching days we have
In August without knowing it sometimes;   35
But Isaac said the day was like a dream,
And praised the Lord, and talked about the breeze.
I made a fair confession of the breeze,
And crowded casually on his thought
The nearness of a profitable nook   40
That I could see. First I was half inclined
To caution him that he was growing old,
But something that was not compassion soon
Made plain the folly of all subterfuge.
Isaac was old, but not so old as that.   45

So I proposed, without an overture,
That we be seated in the shade a while,
And Isaac made no murmur. Soon the talk
Was turned on Archibald, and I began
To feel some premonitions of a kind   50
That only childhood knows; for the old man
Had looked at me and clutched me with his eye,
And asked if I had ever noticed things.
I told him that I could not think of them,
And I knew then, by the frown that left his face   55
Unsatisfied, that I had injured him.
"My good young friend," he said, "you cannot feel
What I have seen so long. You have the eyes—
Oh, yes—but you have not the other things:
The sight within that never will deceive,   60

You do not know—you have no right to know;
The twilight warning of experience,
The singular idea of loneliness,—
These are not yours. But they have long been mine,
And they have shown me now for seven years   65
That Archibald is changing. It is not
So much that he should come to his last hand,
And leave the game, and go the old way down;
But I have known him in and out so long,
And I have seen so much of good in him   70
That other men have shared and have not seen,
And I have gone so far through thick and thin,
Through cold and fire with him, that it brings
To this old heart of mine an ache that you
Have not yet lived enough to know about.   75
But even unto you, with your boy's faith,
Your freedom, and your untried confidence,
A time will come to find out what it means
To know that you are losing what was yours,
To know that you are being left behind;   80
And then the long contempt of innocence—
God bless you, boy!—don't think the worse of it
Because an old man chatters in the shade—
Will all be like a story you have read
In childhood and remembered for the pictures.   85
And when the best friend of your life goes down,
When first you know in him the slackening
That comes, and coming always tells the end,—
Now in a common word that would have passed
Uncaught from any other lips than his,   90
Now in some trivial act of every day,
Done as he might have done it all along
But for a twinging little difference
That bites you like a squirrel's teeth—oh, yes,
Then you will understand it well enough.   95
But oftener it comes in other ways;

It comes without your knowing when it comes;
You know that he is changing, and you know
That he is going—just as I know now
That Archibald is going and that I   100
Am staying. . . . Look at me, my boy,
And when the time shall come for you to see
That I must follow after him, try then
To think of me, to bring me back again,
Just as I was to-day. Think of the place   105
Where we are sitting now, and think of me—
Think of old Isaac as you knew him then,
When you set out with him in August once
To see old Archibald."—The words come back
Almost as Isaac must have uttered them,   110
And there comes with them a dry memory
Of something in my throat that would not move.

If you had asked me then to tell just why
I made so much of Isaac and the things
He said, I should have reached far for an answer;   115
For I knew it was not sorrow that I felt,
Whatever I may have wished it, or tried then
To make myself believe. My mouth was full
Of words, and they would have been comforting
To Isaac, spite of my twelve years, I think;   120
But there was not in me the willingness
To speak them out. Therefore I watched the ground;
And I was wondering what made the Lord
Create a thing so nervous as an ant,
When Isaac, with commendable unrest,   125
Ordained that we should take the road again—
For it was yet three miles to Archibald's,
And one to the first pump. I felt relieved
All over when the old man told me that;
I felt that he had stilled a fear of mine   130
That those extremities of heat and cold

Which he had long gone through with Archibald
Had made the man impervious to both;
But Isaac had a desert somewhere in him,
And at the pump he thanked God for all things   135
That he had put on earth for men to drink,
And he drank well,—so well that I proposed
That we go slowly lest I learn too soon
The bitterness of being left behind,
And all those other things. That was a joke   140
To Isaac, and it pleased him very much;
And that pleased me—for I was twelve years old.

At the end of an hour's walking after that
The cottage of old Archibald appeared.
Little and white and high on a smooth round hill   145
It stood, with hackmatacks and apple-trees
Before it, and a big barn-roof beyond;
And over the place—trees, houses, fields and all—
Hovered an air of still simplicity
And a fragrance of old summers—the old style   150
That lives the while it passes. I dare say
That I was lightly conscious of all this
When Isaac, of a sudden, stopped himself,
And for the long first quarter of a minute
Gazed with incredulous eyes, forgetful quite   155
Of breezes and of me and of all else
Under the scorching sun but a smooth-cut field,
Faint yellow in the distance. I was young,
But there were a few things that I could see,
And this was one of them.—"Well, well!" said he;   160
And "Archibald will be surprised, I think,"
Said I. But all my childhood subtlety
Was lost on Isaac, for he strode along
Like something out of Homer—powerful
And awful on the wayside, so I thought.   165
Also I thought how good it was to be

So near the end of my short-legged endeavor
To keep the pace with Isaac for five miles.

Hardly had we turned in from the main road
When Archibald, with one hand on his back   170
And the other clutching his huge-headed cane,
Came limping down to meet us.—"Well! well! well!"
Said he; and then he looked at my red face,
All streaked with dust and sweat, and shook my hand,
And said it must have been a right smart walk   175
That we had had that day from Tilbury Town.—
"Magnificent," said Isaac; and he told
About the beautiful west wind there was
Which cooled and clarified the atmosphere.
"You must have made it with your legs, I guess,"   180
Said Archibald; and Isaac humored him
With one of those infrequent smiles of his
Which he kept in reserve, apparently,
For Archibald alone. "But why," said he,
"Should Providence have cider in the world   185
If not for such an afternoon as this?"
And Archibald, with a soft light in his eyes,
Replied that if he chose to go down cellar,
There he would find eight barrels—one of which
Was newly tapped, he said, and to his taste   190
An honor to the fruit. Isaac approved
Most heartily of that, and guided us
Forthwith, as if his venerable feet
Were measuring the turf in his own door-yard,
Straight to the open rollway. Down we went,   195
Out of the fiery sunshine to the gloom,
Grateful and half sepulchral, where we found
The barrels, like eight potent sentinels,
Close ranged along the wall. From one of them
A bright pine spile stuck out convincingly,   200
And on the black flat stone, just under it,

Glimmered a late-spilled proof that Archibald
Had spoken from unfeigned experience.
There was a fluted antique water-glass
Close by, and in it, prisoned, or at rest,   205
There was a cricket, of the brown soft sort
That feeds on darkness. Isaac turned him out,
And touched him with his thumb to make him jump,
And then composedly pulled out the plug
With such a practiced hand that scarce a drop   210
Did even touch his fingers. Then he drank
And smacked his lips with a slow patronage
And looked along the line of barrels there
With a pride that may have been forgetfulness:
"I never twist a spigot nowadays,"   215
He said, and raised the glass up to the light,
"But I thank God for orchards." And that glass
Was filled repeatedly for the same hand
Before I thought it worth while to discern
Again that I was young, and that old age,   220
With all his woes, had some advantages.

"Now, Archibald," said Isaac, when we stood
Outside again, "I have it in my mind
That I shall take a sort of little walk—
To stretch my legs and see what you are doing.   225
You stay and rest your back and tell the boy
A story: Tell him all about the time
In Stafford's cabin forty years ago,
When four of us were snowed up for ten days
With only one dried haddock. Tell him all   230
About it, and be wary of your back.
Now I will go along."—I looked up then
At Archibald, and as I looked I saw
The way his nostrils widened once or twice
And then grew narrow. I can hear to-day   235
The way the old man chuckled to himself—

Not wholesomely, not wholly to convince
Another of his mirth,—as I can hear
The lonely sigh that followed.—But at length
He said: "The orchard now's the place for us;   240
We may find something like an apple there,
And we shall have the shade, at any rate."
So there we went and there we laid ourselves
Where the sunlight could not reach us; and I champed
A dozen of worm-blighted astrakhans   245
While Archibald said nothing—merely told
The tale of Stafford's cabin, which was good,
Though "master chilly"—after his own phrase—
Even for a day like that. But other thoughts
Were moving in his mind, imperative,   250
And writhing to be spoken: I could see
The glimmer of them in a glance or two,
Cautious, or else unconscious, that he gave
Over his shoulder: . . . "Stafford and the rest
Would have had no story of their own to tell;   255
They would have left it all for others—yes—
But that's an old song now, and Archibald
And Isaac are old men. Remember, boy,
That we are old. Whatever we have gained,
Or lost, or thrown away, we are old men.   260
You look before you and we look behind,
And we are playing life out in the shadow—
But that's not all of it. The sunshine lights
A good road yet before us if we look,
And we are doing that when least we know it;   265
For both of us are children of the sun,
Like you, and like the weed there at your feet.
The shadow calls us, and it frightens us—
We think; but there's a light behind the stars
And we old fellows who have dared to live,   270
We see it—and we see the other things,
The other things . . . Yes, I have seen it come

These eight years, and these ten years, and I know
Now that it cannot be for very long
That Isaac will be Isaac. You have seen—   275
Young as you are, you must have seen the strange
Uncomfortable habit of the man?
He'll take my nerves and tie them in a knot
Sometimes, and that's not Isaac. I know that—
And I know what it is: I get it here   280
A little, in my knees, and Isaac—here."
The old man shook his head regretfully
And laid his knuckles three times on his forehead.
"That's what it is: Isaac is not quite right.
You see it, but you don't know what it means: 285
The thousand little differences—no,
You do not know them, and it's well you don't;
You'll know them soon enough—God bless you, boy!—
You'll know them, but not all of them—not all.
So think of them as little as you can: 290
There's nothing in them for you, or for me—
But I am old and I must think of them;
I'm in the shadow, but I don't forget
The light, my boy,—the light behind the stars.
Remember that: remember that I said it;   295
And when the time that you think far away
Shall come for you to say it—say it, boy;
Let there be no confusion or distrust
In you, no snarling of a life half lived,
Nor any cursing over broken things   300
That your complaint has been the ruin of.
Live to see clearly and the light will come
To you, and as you need it.—But there, there,
I'm going it again, as Isaac says,
And I'll stop now before you go to sleep.—   305
Only be sure that you growl cautiously,
And always where the shadow may not reach you."

Never shall I forget, long as I live,
The quaint thin crack in Archibald's old voice,
The lonely twinkle in his little eyes,   310
Or the way it made me feel to be with him.
I know I lay and looked for a long time
Down through the orchard and across the road,
Across the river and the sun-scorched hills
That ceased in a blue forest, where the world   315
Ceased with it. Now and then my fancy caught
A flying glimpse of a good life beyond—
Something of ships and sunlight, streets and singing,
Troy falling, and the ages coming back,
And ages coming forward: Archibald   320
And Isaac were good fellows in old clothes
And Agamemnon was a friend of mine;
Ulysses coming home again to shoot
With bows and feathered arrows made another,
And all was as it should be. I was young.   325

So I lay dreaming of what things I would,
Calm and incorrigibly satisfied
With apples and romance and ignorance,
And the floating smoke from Archibald's clay pipe.
There was a stillness over everything,   330
As if the spirit of heat had laid its hand
Upon the world and hushed it; and I felt
Within the mightiness of the white sun
That smote the land around us and wrought out
A fragrance from the trees, a vital warmth   335
And fullness for the time that was to come,
And a glory for the world beyond the forest.
The present and the future and the past,
Isaac and Archibald, the burning bush,
The Trojans and the walls of Jericho,   340
Were beautifully fused; and all went well
Till Archibald began to fret for Isaac

And said it was a master day for sunstroke.
That was enough to make a mummy smile,
I thought; and I remained hilarious,   345
In face of all precedence and respect,
Till Isaac (who had come to us unheard)
Found he had no tobacco, looked at me
Peculiarly, and asked of Archibald
What ailed the boy to make him chirrup so.   350
From that he told us what a blessed world
The Lord had given us.—"But, Archibald,"
He added, with a sweet severity
That made me think of peach-skins and goose-flesh,
"I'm half afraid you cut those oats of yours   355
A day or two before they were well set."
"They were set well enough," said Archibald,—
And I remarked the process of his nose
Before the words came out; "but never mind
Your neighbor's oats: you stay here in the shade   360
And rest yourself while I go find the cards.
We'll have a little game of seven-up
And let the boy keep count."—"We'll have the game,
Assuredly," said Isaac; "and I think
That I will have a draught of cider, also."   365
They marched away together towards the house
And left me to my childish ruminations
Upon the ways of men. I followed them
Down cellar with my fancy, and then left them
For a fairer vision of all things at once   370
That was anon to be destroyed again
By the sound of voices and of heavy feet—
One of the sounds of life that I remember,
Though I forget so many that rang first
As if they were thrown down to me from Sinai.   375

So I remember, even to this day,
Just how they sounded, how they placed themselves,

And how the game went on while I made marks
And crossed them out, and meanwhile made some Trojans.
Likewise I made Ulysses, after Isaac,   380
And a little after Flaxman. Archibald
Was wounded when he found himself left out,
But he had no heroics, and I said so:
I told him that his white beard was too long
And too straight down to be like things in Homer.   385
"Quite so," said Isaac.—"Low," said Archibald;
And he threw down a deuce with a deep grin
That showed his yellow teeth and made me happy.
So they played on till a bell rang from the door,
And Archibald said, "Supper."—After that   390
The old men smoked while I sat watching them
And wondered with all comfort what might come
To me, and what might never come to me;
And when the time came for the long walk home
With Isaac in the twilight, I could see   395
The forest and the sunset and the sky-line,
No matter where it was that I was looking:
The flame beyond the boundary, the music,
The foam and the white ships, and two old men
Were things that would not leave me.—And that night   400
There came to me a dream—a shining one,
With two old angels in it. They had wings,
And they were sitting where a silver light
Suffused them, face to face. The wings of one
Began to palpitate as I approached,   405
But I was yet unseen when a dry voice
Cried thinly, with unpatronizing triumph,
"I've got you, Isaac; high, low, jack, and the game."

Isaac and Archibald have gone their way
To the silence of the loved and well-forgotten.   410
I knew them, and I may have laughed at them;
But there's a laughing that has honor in it,

And I have no regret for light words now.
Rather I think sometimes they may have made
Their sport of me;—but they would not do that,   415
They were too old for that. They were old men,
And I may laugh at them because I knew them.

THE RETURN OF MORGAN AND FINGAL

And there we were together again—
   Together again, we three:
Morgan, Fingal, fiddle, and all,
   They had come for the night with me.

The spirit of joy was in Morgan's wrist,   5
   There were songs in Fingal's throat;
And secure outside, for the spray to drench,
   Was a tossed and empty boat.

And there were the pipes, and there was the punch,
   And somewhere were twelve years;   10
So it came, in the manner of things unsought,
   That a quick knock vexed our ears.

The night wind hovered and shrieked and snarled,
   And I heard Fingal swear;
Then I opened the door—but I found no more   15
   Than a chalk-skinned woman there.

I looked, and at last, "What is it?" I said—
   "What is it that we can do?"
But never a word could I get from her
   But "You—you three—it is you!"   20

Now the sense of a crazy speech like that
    Was more than a man could make;
So I said, "But we—we are what, we three?"
    And I saw the creature shake.

"Be quick!" she cried, "for I left her dead—   25
    And I was afraid to come;
But you, you three—God made it be—
    Will ferry the dead girl home.

"Be quick! be quick!—but listen to that
    Who is it that makes it?—hark!"   30
But I heard no more than a knocking splash
    And a wind that shook the dark.

"It is only the wind that blows," I said,
    "And the boat that rocks outside."
And I watched her there, and I pitied her there—   35
    "Be quick! be quick!" she cried.

She cried it so loud that her voice went in
    To find where my two friends were;
So Morgan came, and Fingal came,
    And out we went with her.   40

'T was a lonely way for a man to take
    And a tedious way for three;
And over the water, and all day long,
    They had come for the night with me.

But the girl was dead, as the woman had said,   45
    And the best we could see to do
Was to lay her aboard. The north wind roared,
    And into the night we flew.

Four of us living and one for a ghost,
  Furrowing crest and swell,   50
Through the surge and the dark, for that faint far spark,
  We ploughed with Azrael.

Three of us ruffled and one gone mad,
  Crashing to south we went;
And three of us there were too spattered to care   55
  What this late sailing meant.

So down we steered and along we tore
  Through the flash of the midnight foam:
Silent enough to be ghosts on guard,
  We ferried the dead girl home.   60

We ferried her down to the voiceless wharf,
  And we carried her up to the light;
And we left the two to the father there,
  Who counted the coals that night.

Then back we steered through the foam again,   65
  But our thoughts were fast and few;
And all we did was to crowd the surge
  And to measure the life we knew;—

Till at last we came where a dancing gleam
  Skipped out to us, we three,—   70
And the dark wet mooring pointed home
  Like a finger from the sea.

Then out we pushed the teetering skiff
  And in we drew to the stairs;
And up we went, each man content   75
  With a life that fed no cares.

Fingers were cold and feet were cold,
    And the tide was cold and rough;
But the light was warm, and the room was warm,
    And the world was good enough.   80

And there were the pipes, and there was the punch,
    More shrewd than Satan's tears:
Fingal had fashioned it, all by himself,
    With a craft that comes of years.

And there we were together again—   85
    Together again, we three:
Morgan, Fingal, fiddle, and all,
    They were there for the night with me.

AUNT IMOGEN

Aunt Imogen was coming, and therefore
The children—Jane, Sylvester, and Young George—
Were eyes and ears; for there was only one
Aunt Imogen to them in the whole world,
And she was in it only for four weeks   5
In fifty-two. But those great bites of time
Made all September a Queen's Festival;
And they would strive, informally, to make
The most of them.—The mother understood,
And wisely stepped away. Aunt Imogen   10
Was there for only one month in the year,
While she, the mother,—she was always there;
And that was what made all the difference.
She knew it must be so, for Jane had once
Expounded it to her so learnedly   15

That she had looked away from the child's eyes
And thought; and she had thought of many things.

There was a demonstration every time
Aunt Imogen appeared, and there was more
Than one this time. And she was at a loss   20
Just how to name the meaning of it all:
It puzzled her to think that she could be
So much to any crazy things alive—
Even to her sister's little savages
Who knew no better than to be themselves;   25
But in the midst of her glad wonderment
She found herself besieged and overcome
By two tight arms and one tumultuous head,
And therewith half bewildered and half pained
By the joy she felt and by the sudden love   30
That proved itself in childhood's honest noise.
Jane, by the wings of sex, had reached her first;
And while she strangled her, approvingly,
Sylvester thumped his drum and Young George howled.—
But finally, when all was rectified,   35
And she had stilled the clamor of Young George
By letting him go "pig-back" through the hall,
They went together into the old room
That looked across the fields; and Imogen
Gazed out with a girl's gladness in her eyes,   40
Happy to know that she was back once more
Where there were those who knew her, and at last
Had gloriously got away again
From cabs and clattered asphalt for a while;
And there she sat and talked and looked and laughed   45
And made the mother and the children laugh.
Aunt Imogen made everybody laugh.

There was the feminine paradox—that she
Who had so little sunshine for herself

Should have so much for others. How it was   50
That she could make, and feel for making it,
So much of joy for them, and all along
Be covering, like a scar, the while she smiled,
That hungering incompleteness and regret—
That passionate ache for something of her own,   55
For something of herself—she never knew.
She knew that she could seem to make them all
Believe there was no other part of her
Than her persistent happiness; but the why
And how she did not know. Still none of them   60
Could have a thought that she was living down—
Almost as if regret were criminal,
So proud it was and yet so profitless—
The penance of a dream, and that was good:
Even her big bewhiskered brother Giles   65
Had called her in his letter, not long since,
A superannuated pretty girl;
And she, to do the thing most adequate
Had posted back sarcastic sheets enough
To keep the beast in humor for a month.   70
But her sister Jane—the mother of little Jane,
Sylvester, and Young George—may, after all,
Have known; for she was—well, she was a woman.

Young George, however, did not yield himself
To nourish the false hunger of a ghost   75
That made no good return. He saw too much:
The accumulated wisdom of his years
Had so conclusively made plain to him
The permanent profusion of a world
Where everybody might have everything   80
To do, and almost everything to eat,
That he was jubilantly satisfied
And all unthwarted by adversity.
Young George knew things. The world, he had found out,

Was a good place, and life was a good game—   85
Particularly when Aunt Imogen
Was in it. And one day it came to pass—
One rainy day when she was holding him
And rocking him—that he, in his own right,
Took it upon himself to tell her so;   90
And something in his way of telling it—
The language, or the tone, or something else—
Gripped like a baby's fingers on her throat,
And then went feeling through as if to make
A plaything of her heart. Such undeserved   95
And unsophisticated confidence
Went mercilessly home; and had she sat
Before a looking glass, the deeps of it
Could not have shown more clearly to her then
Than one thought-mirrored little glimpse had shown   100
The pang that wrenched her face and filled her eyes
With anguish and intolerable mist.
The blow that she had vaguely thrust aside
Like fright so many times had found her now:
Clean-thrust and final it had come to her   105
From a child's lips at last, as it had come
Never before, and as it might be felt
Never again. Some grief, like some delight,
Stings hard but once: to custom after that
The rapture or the pain submits itself,   110
And we are wiser than we were before.
And Imogen was wiser; though at first
Her dream-defeating wisdom was indeed
A thankless heritage: there was no sweet,
No bitter now; nor was there anything   115
To make a daily meaning for her life—
Till truth, like Harlequin, leapt out somehow
From ambush and threw sudden savor to it—
But the blank taste of time. There were no dreams,
No phantoms in her future any more: 120

One clinching revelation of what was,
One by-flash of irrevocable chance,
Had acridly but honestly foretold
The mystical fulfillment of a life
That might have once . . . But that was all gone by: 125
There was no need of reaching back for that:
The triumph was not hers: there was no love
Save borrowed love: there was no might have been.

But there was yet Young George—and he had gone
Conveniently to sleep, like a good boy;   130
And there was yet Sylvester with his drum,
And there was frowzle-headed little Jane;
And there was Jane the sister, and the mother,—
Her sister, and the mother of them all.
They were not hers, not even one of them: 135
She was not born to be so much as that,
For she was born to be Aunt Imogen.
Now she could see the truth and look at it;
Now she could make stars out where once had palled
A future's emptiness; now she could share   140
With others—ah, the others!—to the end
The largess of a woman who could smile;
Now it was hers to dance the folly down,
And all the murmuring; now it was hers
To be Aunt Imogen.—So, when Young George   145
Woke up and blinked at her with his big eyes,
And smiled to see the way she blinked at him,
'T was only in old concord with the stars
That she took hold of him and held him close,
Close to herself, and crushed him till he laughed.   150

THE KLONDIKE

Never mind the day we left, or the way the women clung to us;
All we need now is the last way they looked at us.
Never mind the twelve men there amid the cheering—
Twelve men or one man, 't will soon be all the same;
For this is what we know: we are five men together,   5
Five left o' twelve men to find the golden river.

Far we came to find it out, but the place was here for all of us;
Far, far we came, and here we have the last of us.
We that were the front men, we that would be early,
We that had the faith, and the triumph in our eyes: 10
We that had the wrong road, twelve men together,—
Singing when the devil sang to find the golden river.

Say the gleam was not for us, but never say we doubted it;
Say the wrong road was right before we followed it.
We that were the front men, fit for all forage,—   15
Say that while we dwindle we are front men still;
For this is what we know to-night: we're starving here together—
Starving on the wrong road to find the golden river.

Wrong, we say, but wait a little: hear him in the corner there;
He knows more than we, and he'll tell us if we listen there—   20
He that fought the snow-sleep less than all the others
Stays awhile yet, and he knows where he stays:
Foot and hand a frozen clout, brain a freezing feather,
Still he's here to talk with us and to the golden river.

"Flow," he says, "and flow along, but you cannot flow away from
    us;   25
All the world's ice will never keep you far from us;

Every man that heeds your call takes the way that leads him—
The one way that's his way, and lives his own life:
Starve or laugh, the game goes on, and on goes the river;
Gold or no, they go their way—twelve men together.   30

"Twelve," he says, "who sold their shame for a lure you call too
    fair for them—
You that laugh and flow to the same word that urges them:
Twelve who left the old town shining in the sunset,
Left the weary street and the small safe days:
Twelve who knew but one way out, wide the way or narrow: 35
Twelve who took the frozen chance and laid their lives on
    yellow.

"Flow by night and flow by day, nor ever once be seen by them;
Flow, freeze, and flow, till time shall hide the bones of them;
Laugh and wash their names away, leave them all forgotten,
Leave the old town to crumble where it sleeps;   40
Leave it there as they have left it, shining in the valley,—
Leave the town to crumble down and let the women marry.

"Twelve of us or five," he says, "we know the night is on us
    now:
Five while we last, and we may as well be thinking now:
Thinking each his own thought, knowing, when the light
    comes,   45
Five left or none left, the game will not be lost.
Crouch or sleep, we go the way, the last way together:
Five or none, the game goes on, and on goes the river.

"For after all that we have done and all that we have failed
    to do,
Life will be life and the world will have its work to do: 50
Every man who follows us will heed in his own fashion
The calling and the warning and the friends who do not know:

Each will hold an icy knife to punish his heart's lover,
And each will go the frozen way to find the golden river."

There you hear him, all he says, and the last we'll ever get from
    him.   55
Now he wants to sleep, and that will be the best for him.
Let him have his own way—no, you needn't shake him—
Your own turn will come, so let the man sleep.
For this is what we know: we are stalled here together—
Hands and feet and hearts of us, to find the golden river.   60

And there's a quicker way than sleep? . . . Never mind the
    looks of him:
All he needs now is a finger on the eyes of him.
You there on the left hand, reach a little over—
Shut the stars away, or he'll see them all night:
He'll see them all night and he'll see them all to-morrow,   65
Crawling down the frozen sky, cold and hard and yellow.

Won't you move an inch or two—to keep the stars away from
    him?
—No, he won't move, and there's no need of asking him.
Never mind the twelve men, never mind the women;
Three while we last, we'll let them all go;   70
And we'll hold our thoughts north while we starve here together,
Looking each his own way to find the golden river.

THE GROWTH OF "LORRAINE"

I

While I stood listening, discreetly dumb,
Lorraine was having the last word with me:
"I know," she said, "I know it, but you see
Some creatures are born fortunate, and some
Are born to be found out and overcome,—   5

Born to be slaves, to let the rest go free;
And if I'm one of them (and I must be)
You may as well forget me and go home.

"You tell me not to say these things, I know,
But I should never try to be content: 10
I've gone too far; the life would be too slow.
Some could have done it—some girls have the stuff;
But I can't do it: I don't know enough.
I'm going to the devil."—And she went.

II

I did not half believe her when she said   15
That I should never hear from her again;
Nor when I found a letter from Lorraine,
Was I surprised or grieved at what I read:
"Dear friend, when you find this, I shall be dead.
You are too far away to make me stop.   20
They say that one drop—think of it, one drop!—
Will be enough,—but I'll take five instead.

"You do not frown because I call you friend,
For I would have you glad that I still keep
Your memory, and even at the end—   25
Impenitent, sick, shattered—cannot curse
The love that flings, for better or for worse,
This worn-out, cast-out flesh of mine to sleep."

THE SAGE

Foreguarded and unfevered and serene,
Back to the perilous gates of Truth he went—
Back to fierce wisdom and the Orient,
To the Dawn that is, that shall be, and has been:

Previsioned of the madness and the mean,   5
He stood where Asia, crowned with ravishment,
The curtain of Love's inner shrine had rent,
And after had gone scarred by the Unseen.

There at his touch there was a treasure chest,
And in it was a gleam, but not of gold;   10
And on it, like a flame, these words were scrolled:
"I keep the mintage of Eternity.
Who comes to take one coin may take the rest,
And all may come—but not without the key."

ERASMUS

When he protested, not too solemnly,
That for a world's achieving maintenance
The crust of overdone divinity
Lacked aliment, they called it recreance;
And when he chose through his own glass to scan   5
Sick Europe, and reduced, unyieldingly,
The monk within the cassock to the man
Within the monk, they called it heresy.

And when he made so perilously bold
As to be scattered forth in black and white,   10
Good fathers looked askance at him and rolled
Their inward eyes in anguish and affright;
There were some of them did shake at what was told,
And they shook best who knew that he was right.

THE WOMAN AND THE WIFE

I—*The Explanation*

"You thought we knew," she said, "but we were wrong. 2
This we can say, the rest we do not say;
Nor do I let you throw yourself away
Because you love me. Let us both be strong,
And we shall find in sorrow, before long, 5
Only the price Love ruled that we should pay:
The dark is at the end of every day,
And silence is the end of every song.

"You ask me for one proof that I speak right,
But I can answer only what I know; 10
You look for just one lie to make black white,
But I can tell you only what is true—
God never made me for the wife of you.
This we can say,—believe me! . . . Tell me so!"

II—*The Anniversary*

"Give me the truth, whatever it may be. 15
You thought we knew, now tell me what you miss:
You are the one to tell me what it is—
You are a man, and you have married me.
What is it worth to-night that you can see
More marriage in the dream of one dead kiss 20
Than in a thousand years of life like this?
Passion has turned the lock, Pride keeps the key.

"Whatever I have said or left unsaid,
Whatever I have done or left undone,—
Tell me. Tell me the truth. . . . Are you afraid? 25

Do you think that Love was ever fed with lies
But hunger lived thereafter in his eyes?
Do you ask me to take moonlight for the sun?"

THE BOOK OF ANNANDALE

I

Partly to think, more to be left alone,
George Annandale said something to his friends—
A word or two, brusque, but yet smoothed enough
To suit their funeral gaze—and went upstairs;
And there, in the one room that he could call   5
His own, he found a kind of meaningless
Annoyance in the mute familiar things
That filled it; for the grate's monotonous gleam
Was not the gleam that he had known before,
The books were not the books that used to be,   10
The place was not the place. There was a lack
Of something; and the certitude of death
Itself, as with a furtive questioning,
Hovered, and he could not yet understand.
He knew that she was gone—there was no need   15
Of any argued proof to tell him that,
For they had buried her that afternoon,
Under the leaves and snow; and still there was
A doubt, a pitiless doubt, a plunging doubt,
That struck him, and upstartled when it struck,   20
The vision, the old thought in him. There was
A lack, and one that wrenched him; but it was
Not that—not that. There was a present sense
Of something indeterminably near—
The soul-clutch of a prescient emptiness   25
That would not be foreboding. And if not,

What then?—or was it anything at all?
Yes, it was something—it was everything—
But what was everything? or anything?

Tired of time, bewildered, he sat down;   30
But in his chair he kept on wondering
That he should feel so desolately strange
And yet—for all he knew that he had lost
More of the world than most men ever win—
So curiously calm. And he was left   35
Unanswered and unsatisfied: there came
No clearer meaning to him than had come
Before; the old abstraction was the best
That he could find, the farthest he could go;
To that was no beginning and no end—   40
No end that he could reach. So he must learn
To live the surest and the largest life
Attainable in him, would he divine
The meaning of the dream and of the words
That he had written, without knowing why,   45
On sheets that he had bound up like a book
And covered with red leather. There it was—
There in his desk, the record he had made,
The spiritual plaything of his life:
There were the words no eyes had ever seen   50
Save his; there were the words that were not made
For glory or for gold. The pretty wife
Whom he had loved and lost had not so much
As heard of them. They were not made for her.
His love had been so much the life of her,   55
And hers had been so much the life of him,
That any wayward phrasing on his part
Would have had no moment. Neither had lived enough
To know the book, albeit one of them
Had grown enough to write it. There it was,   60

However, though he knew not why it was:
There was the book, but it was not for her,
For she was dead. And yet, there was the book

Thus would his fancy circle out and out,
And out and in again, till he would make   65
As if with a large freedom to crush down
Those under-thoughts. He covered with his hands
His tired eyes, and waited: he could hear—
Or partly feel and hear, mechanically—
The sound of talk, with now and then the steps   70
And skirts of some one scudding on the stairs,
Forgetful of the nerveless funeral feet
That she had brought with her; and more than once
There came to him a call as of a voice—
A voice of love returning—but not hers.   75
Whose he knew not, nor dreamed; nor did he know,
Nor did he dream, in his blurred loneliness
Of thought, what all the rest might think of him.

For it had come at last, and she was gone
With all the vanished women of old time,—   80
And she was never coming back again.
Yes, they had buried her that afternoon,
Under the frozen leaves and the cold earth,
Under the leaves and snow. The flickering week,
The sharp and certain day, and the long drowse   85
Were over, and the man was left alone.
He knew the loss—Therefore it puzzled him
That he should sit so long there as he did,
And bring the whole thing back—the love, the trust,
The pallor, the poor face, and the faint way   90
She last had looked at him—and yet not weep,
Or even choose to look about the room
To see how sad it was; and once or twice
He winked and pinched his eyes against the flame

And hoped there might be tears. But hope was all,   95
And all to him was nothing: he was lost.
And yet he was not lost: he was astray—
Out of his life and in another life;
And in the stillness of this other life
He wondered and he drowsed. He wondered when   100
It was, and wondered if it ever was
On earth that he had known the other face—
The searching face, the eloquent, strange face—
That with a sightless beauty looked at him
And with a speechless promise uttered words   105
That were not the world's words, or any kind
That he had known before. What was it, then?
What was it held him—fascinated him?
Why should he not be human? He could sigh,
And he could even groan,—but what of that?   110
There was no grief left in him. Was he glad?

Yet how could he be glad, or reconciled,
Or anything but wretched and undone?
How could he be so frigid and inert—
So like a man with water in his veins   115
Where blood had been a little while before?
How could he sit shut in there like a snail?
What ailed him? What was on him? Was he glad?
Over and over again the question came,
Unanswered and unchanged,—and there he was.   120
But what in heaven's name did it all mean?
If he had lived as other men had lived,
If home had ever shown itself to be
The counterfeit that others had called home,
Then to this undivined resource of his   125
There were some key; but now . . . Philosophy?
Yes, he could reason in a kind of way
That he was glad for Miriam's release—
Much as he might be glad to see his friends

Laid out around him with their grave-clothes on,   130
And this life done for them; but something else
There was that foundered reason, overwhelmed it,
And with a chilled, intuitive rebuff
Beat back the self-cajoling sophistries
That his half-tutored thought would half-project.   135

What was it, then? Had he become transformed
And hardened through long watches and long grief
Into a loveless, feelingless dead thing
That brooded like a man, breathed like a man,—
Did everything but ache? And was a day   140
To come some time when feeling should return
Forever to drive off that other face—
The lineless, indistinguishable face—
That once had thrilled itself between his own
And hers there on the pillow,—and again   145
Between him and the coffin-lid had flashed
Like fate before it closed,—and at the last
Had come, as it should seem, to stay with him,
Bidden or not? He were a stranger then,
Foredrowsed awhile by some deceiving draught   150
Of poppied anguish, to the covert grief
And the stark loneliness that waited him,
And for the time were cursedly endowed
With a dull trust that shammed indifference
To knowing there would be no touch again   155
Of her small hand on his, no silencing
Of her quick lips on his, no feminine
Completeness and love-fragrance in the house,
No sound of some one singing any more,
No smoothing of slow fingers on his hair,   160
No shimmer of pink slippers on brown tiles.

But there was nothing, nothing, in all that:
He had not fooled himself so much as that;

He might be dreaming or he might be sick,
But not like that. There was no place for fear, 165
No reason for remorse. There was the book
That he had made, though. . . . It might be the book;
Perhaps he might find something in the book;
But no, there could be nothing there at all—
He knew it word for word; but what it meant— 170
He was not sure that he had written it
For what it meant; and he was not quite sure
That he had written it;—more likely it
Was all a paper ghost. . . . But the dead wife
Was real: he knew that, for he had been 175
To see them bury her; and he had seen
The flowers and the snow and the stripped limbs
Of trees; and he had heard the preacher pray;
And he was back again, and he was glad.
Was he a brute? No, he was not a brute: 180
He was a man—like any other man:
He had loved and married his wife Miriam,
They had lived a little while in paradise
And she was gone; and that was all of it.

But no, not all of it—not all of it: 185
There was the book again; something in that
Pursued him, overpowered him, put out
The futile strength of all his whys and wheres,
And left him unintelligibly numb—
Too numb to care for anything but rest. 190
It must have been a curious kind of book
That he had made: it was a drowsy book
At any rate. The very thought of it
Was like the taste of some impossible drink—
A taste that had no taste, but for all that 195
Had mixed with it a strange thought-cordial,
So potent that it somehow killed in him
The ultimate need of doubting any more—

Of asking any more. Did he but live
The life that he must live, there were no more   200
To seek.—The rest of it was on the way.

Still there was nothing, nothing, in all this—
Nothing that he cared now to reconcile
With reason or with sorrow. All he knew
For certain was that he was tired out: 205
His flesh was heavy and his blood beat small;
Something supreme had been wrenched out of him
As if to make vague room for something else.
He had been through too much. Yes, he would stay
There where he was and rest.—And there he stayed;   210
The daylight became twilight, and he stayed;
The flame and the face faded, and he slept.
And they had buried her that afternoon,
Under the tight-screwed lid of a long box,
Under the earth, under the leaves and snow.   215

II—*Damaris*

Look where she would, feed conscience how she might,
There was but one way now for Damaris—
One straight way that was hers, hers to defend,
At hand, imperious. But the nearness of it,
The flesh-bewildering simplicity,   220
And the plain strangeness of it, thrilled again
That wretched little quivering single string
Which yielded not, but held her to the place
Where now for five triumphant years had slept
The flameless dust of Argan.—He was gone,   225
The good man she had married long ago;
And she had lived, and living she had learned,
And surely there was nothing to regret:
Much happiness had been for each of them,
And they had been like lovers to the last: 230
And after that, and long, long after that,

Her tears had washed out more of widowed grief
Than smiles had ever told of other joy.—
But could she, looking back, find anything
That should return to her in the new time,   235
And with relentless magic uncreate
This temple of new love where she had thrown
Dead sorrow on the altar of new life?
Only one thing, only one thread was left;
When she broke that, when reason snapped it off,   240
And once for all, baffled, the grave let go
The trivial hideous hold it had on her,—
Then she were free, free to be what she would,
Free to be what she was.—And yet she stayed,
Leashed, as it were, and with a cobweb strand,   245
Close to a tombstone—maybe to starve there.

But why to starve? And why stay there at all?
Why not make one good leap and then be done
Forever and at once with Argan's ghost
And all such outworn churchyard servitude?   250
For it was Argan's ghost that held the string,
And her sick fancy that held Argan's ghost—
Held it and pitied it. She laughed, almost,
There for the moment; but her strained eyes filled
With tears, and she was angry for those tears—   255
Angry at first, then proud, then sorry for them.
So she grew calm; and after a vain chase
For thoughts more vain, she questioned of herself
What measure of primeval doubts and fears
Were still to be gone through that she might win   260
Persuasion of her strength and of herself
To be what she could see that she must be,
No matter where the ghost was.—And the more
She lived, the more she came to recognize
That something out of her thrilled ignorance   265
Was luminously, proudly being born,

And thereby proving, thought by forward thought,
The prowess of its image; and she learned
At length to look right on to the long days
Before her without fearing. She could watch   270
The coming course of them as if they were
No more than birds, that slowly, silently,
And irretrievably should wing themselves
Uncounted out of sight. And when he came
Again she should be free—she would be free.   275
Else, when he looked at her she must look down,
Defeated, and malignly dispossessed
Of what was hers to prove and in the proving
Wisely to consecrate. And if the plague
Of that perverse defeat should come to be—   280
If at that sickening end she were to find
Herself to be the same poor prisoner
That he had found at first—then she must lose
All sight and sound of him, she must abjure
All possible thought of him; for he would go   285
So far and for so long from her that love—
Even a love like his, exiled enough,
Might for another's touch be born again—
Born to be lost and starved for and not found;
Or, at the next, the second wretchedest,   290
It might go mutely flickering down and out,
And on some incomplete and piteous day,
Some perilous day to come, she might at last
Learn, with a noxious freedom, what it is
To be at peace with ghosts. Then were the blow   295
Thrice deadlier than any kind of death
Could ever be: to know that she had won
The truth too late—there were the dregs indeed
Of wisdom, and of love the final thrust
Unmerciful; and there where now did lie   300
So plain before her the straight radiance
Of what was her appointed way to take,

Were only the bleak ruts of an old road
That stretched ahead and faded and lay far
Through deserts of unconscionable years.   305

But vampire thoughts like these confessed the doubt
That love denied; and once, if never again,
They should be turned away. They might come back—
More craftily, perchance, they might come back—
And with a spirit-thirst insatiable   310
Finish the strength of her; but now, to-day
She would have none of them. She knew that love
Was true, that he was true, that she was true;
And should a death-bed snare that she had made
So long ago be stretched inexorably   315
Through all her life, only to be unspun
With her last breathing? And were bats and threads,
Accursedly devised with watered gules,
To be Love's heraldry? What were it worth
To live and to find out that life were life   320
But for an unrequited incubus
Of outlawed shame that would not be thrown down
Till she had thrown down fear and overcome
The woman that was yet so much of her
That she might yet go mad? What were it worth   325
To live, to linger and to be condemned
In her submission to a common thought
That clogged itself and made of its first faith
Its last impediment? What augured it,
Now in this quick beginning of new life,   330
To clutch the sunlight and be feeling back,
Back with a scared fantastic fearfulness,
To touch, not knowing why, the vexed-up ghost
Of what was gone?

        Yes, there was Argan's face,
Pallid and pinched and ruinously marked   335
With big pathetic bones; there were his eyes,

Quiet and large, fixed wistfully on hers;
And there, close-pressed again within her own,
Quivered his cold thin fingers. And, ah! yes,
There were the words, those dying words again,   340
And hers that answered when she promised him.
Promised him? . . . yes. And had she known the truth
Of what she felt that he should ask her that,
And had she known the love that was to be,
God knew that she could not have told him then.   345
But then she knew it not, nor thought of it;
There was no need of it; nor was there need
Of any problematic support
Whereto to cling while she convinced herself
That love's intuitive utility,   350
Inexorably merciful, had proved
That what was human was unpermanent
And what was flesh was ashes. She had told
Him then that she would love no other man,
That there was not another man on earth   355
Whom she could ever love, or who could make
So much as a love thought go through her brain;
And he had smiled. And just before he died
His lips had made as if to say something—
Something that passed unwhispered with his breath,   360
Out of her reach, out of all quest of it.
And then, could she have known enough to know
The meaning of her grief, the folly of it,
The faithlessness and the proud anguish of it,
There might be now no threads to punish her,   365
No vampire thoughts to suck the coward blood,
The life, the very soul of her.

                                    Yes, Yes,
They might come back. . . . But why should they come
    back?
Why was it she had suffered? Why had she

Struggled and grown these years to demonstrate 370
That close without those hovering clouds of gloom
And through them here and there forever gleamed
The Light itself, the life, the love, the glory,
Which was of its own radiance good proof
That all the rest was darkness and blind sight? 375
And who was *she?* The woman she had known—
The woman she had petted and called "I"—
The woman she had pitied, and at last
Commiserated for the most abject
And persecuted of all womankind,— 380
Could it be she that had sought out the way
To measure and thereby to quench in her
The woman's fear—the fear of her not fearing?
A nervous little laugh that lost itself,
Like logic in a dream, fluttered her thoughts 385
An instant there that ever she should ask
What she might then have told so easily—
So easily that Annandale had frowned,
Had he been given wholly to be told
The truth of what had never been before 390
So passionately, so inevitably
Confessed.

        For she could see from where she sat
The sheets that he had bound up like a book
And covered with red leather; and her eyes
Could see between the pages of the book, 395
Though her eyes, like them, were closed. And she could read
As well as if she had them in her hand,
What he had written on them long ago,—
Six years ago, when he was waiting for her.
She might as well have said that she could see 400
The man himself, as once he would have looked
Had she been there to watch him while he wrote
Those words, and all for her. . . . For her whose face

Had flashed itself, prophetic and unseen,
But not unspirited, between the life   405
That would have been without her and the life
That he had gathered up like frozen roots
Out of a grave-clod lying at his feet,
Unconsciously, and as unconsciously
Transplanted and revived. He did not know   410
The kind of life that he had found, nor did
He doubt, not knowing it; but well he knew
That it was life—new life, and that the old
Might then with unimprisoned wings go free,
Onward and all along to its own light,   415
Through the appointed shadow.

                        While she gazed
Upon it there she felt within herself
The growing of a newer consciousness—
The pride of something fairer than her first
Outclamoring of interdicted thought   420
Had ever quite foretold; and all at once
There quivered and requivered through her flesh,
Like music, like the sound of an old song,
Triumphant, love-remembered murmurings
Of what for passion's innocence had been   425
Too mightily, too perilously hers,
Ever to be reclaimed and realized
Until to-day. To-day she could throw off
The burden that had held her down so long,
And she could stand upright, and she could see   430
The way to take, with eyes that had in them
No gleam but of the spirit. Day or night,
No matter; she could see what was to see—
All that had been till now shut out from her,
The service, the fulfillment, and the truth,   435
And thus the cruel wiseness of it all.

So Damaris, more like than anything
To one long prisoned in a twilight cave
With hovering bats for all companionship,
And after time set free to fight the sun,   440
Laughed out, so glad she was to recognize
The test of what had been, through all her folly,
The courage of her conscience; for she knew,
Now on a late-flushed autumn afternoon
That else had been too bodeful of dead things   445
To be endured with aught but the same old
Inert, self-contradicted martyrdom
Which she had known so long, that she could look
Right forward through the years, nor any more
Shrink with a cringing prescience to behold   450
The glitter of dead summer on the grass,
Or the brown-glimmered crimson of still trees
Across the intervale where flashed along,
Black-silvered, the cold river. She had found,
As if by some transcendent freakishness   455
Of reason, the glad life that she had sought
Where naught but obvious clouds could ever be—
Clouds to put out the sunlight from her eyes,
And to put out the love-light from her soul.
But they were gone—now they were all gone;   460
And with a whimsied pathos, like the mist
Of grief that clings to new-found happiness
Hard wrought, she might have pity for the small
Defeated quest of them that brushed her sight
Like flying lint—lint that had once been thread. . . .   465

Yes, like an anodyne, the voice of him,
There were the words that he had made for her,
For her alone. The more she thought of them
The more she lived them, and the more she knew
The life-grip and the pulse of warm strength in them.   470

They were the first and last of words to her,
And there was in them a far questioning
That had for long been variously at work,
Divinely and elusively at work,
With her, and with the grave that had been hers;   475
They were eternal words, and they diffused
A flame of meaning that men's lexicons
Had never kindled; they were choral words
That harmonized with love's enduring chords
Like wisdom with release; triumphant words   480
That rang like elemental orisons
Through ages out of ages; words that fed
Love's hunger in the spirit; words that smote;
Thrilled words that echoed, and barbed words that clung;—
And every one of them was like a friend   485
Whose obstinate fidelity, well tried,
Had found at last and irresistibly
The way to her close conscience, and thereby
Revealed the unsubstantial Nemesis
That she had clutched and shuddered at so long;   490
And every one of them was like a real
And ringing voice, clear toned and absolute,
But of a love-subdued authority
That uttered thrice the plain significance
Of what had else been generously vague   495
And indolently true. It may have been
The triumph and the magic of the soul,
Unspeakably revealed, that finally
Had reconciled the grim probationing
Of wisdom with unalterable faith,   500
But she could feel—not knowing what it was,
For the sheer freedom of it—a new joy
That humanized the latent wizardry
Of his prophetic voice and put for it
The man within the music.

                                    So it came   505
To pass, like many a long-compelled emprise
That with its first accomplishment almost
Annihilates its own severity,
That she could find, whenever she might look,
The certified achievement of a love   510
That had endured, self-guarded and supreme,
To the glad end of all that wavering;
And she could see that now the flickering world
Of autumn was awake with sudden bloom,
New-born, perforce, of a slow bourgeoning.   515
And she had found what more than half had been
The grave-deluded, flesh-bewildered fear
Which men and women struggle to call faith,
To be the paid progression to an end
Whereat she knew the foresight and the strength   520
To glorify the gift of what was hers,
To vindicate the truth of what she was.
And had it come to her so suddenly?
There was a pity and a weariness
In asking that, and a great needlessness;   525
For now there were no wretched quivering strings
That held her to the churchyard any more:
There were no thoughts that flapped themselves like bats
Around her any more. The shield of love
Was clean, and she had paid enough to learn   530
How it had always been so. And the truth,
Like silence after some far victory,
Had come to her, and she had found it out
As if it were a vision, a thing born
So suddenly!—just as a flower is born,   535
Or as a world is born—so suddenly.

SAINTE-NITOUCHE

Though not for common praise of him,
  Nor yet for pride or charity,
Still would I make to Vanderberg
  One tribute for his memory:

One honest warrant of a friend   5
  Who found with him that flesh was grass—
Who neither blamed him in defect
  Nor marveled how it came to pass;

Or why it ever was that he—
  That Vanderberg, of all good men,   10
Should lose himself to find himself,
  Straightway to lose himself again.

For we had buried Sainte-Nitouche,
  And he had said to me that night:
"Yes, we have laid her in the earth,   15
  But what of that?" And he was right.

And he had said: "We have a wife,
  We have a child, we have a church;
'T would be a scurrilous way out
  If we should leave them in the lurch.   20

"That's why I have you here with me
  To-night: you know a talk may take
The place of bromide, cyanide,
  Et cetera. For heaven's sake,

"Why do you look at me like that?   25
  What have I done to freeze you so?

Dear man, you see where friendship means
  A few things yet that you don't know;

"And you see partly why it is
  That I am glad for what is gone:
For Sainte-Nitouche and for the world
  In me that followed. What lives on—   30

"Well, here you have it: here at home—
  For even home will yet return.
You know the truth is on my side,
  And that will make the embers burn.   35

"I see them brighten while I speak,
  I see them flash,—and they are mine!
You do not know them, but I do:
  I know the way they used to shine.   40

"And I know more than I have told
  Of other life that is to be:
I shall have earned it when it comes,
  And when it comes I shall be free.

"Not as I was before she came,   45
  But farther on for having been
The servitor, the slave of her—
  The fool, you think. But there's your sin—

"Forgive me!—and your ignorance:
  Could you but have the vision here   50
That I have, you would understand
  As I do that all ways are clear

"For those who dare to follow them
  With earnest eyes and honest feet.
But Sainte-Nitouche has made the way   55
  For me, and I shall find it sweet.

"Sweet with a bitter sting left?—Yes,
  Bitter enough, God knows, at first;
But there are more steep ways than one
  To make the best look like the worst;   60

"And here is mine—the dark and hard,
  For me to follow, trust, and hold:
And worship, so that I may leave
  No broken story to be told.

"Therefore I welcome what may come,   65
  Glad for the days, the nights, the years."—
An upward flash of ember-flame
  Revealed the gladness in his tears.

"You see them, but you know," said he,
  "Too much to be incredulous: 70
You know the day that makes us wise,
  The moment that makes fools of us.

"So I shall follow from now on
  The road that she has found for me:
The dark and starry way that leads   75
  Right upward, and eternally.

"Stumble at first? I may do that;
  And I may grope, and hate the night;
But there's a guidance for the man
  Who stumbles upward for the light,   80

"And I shall have it all from her,
  The foam-born child of innocence.
I feel you smiling while I speak,
  But that's of little consequence;

"For when we learn that we may find   85
 The truth where others miss the mark,
What is it worth for us to know
 That friends are smiling in the dark?

"Could we but share the lonely pride
 Of knowing, all would then be well;   90
But knowledge often writes itself
 In flaming words we cannot spell.

"And I, who have my work to do,
 Look forward; and I dare to see,
Far stretching and all mountainous,   95
 God's pathway through the gloom for me."

I found so little to say then
 That I said nothing.—"Say good-night,"
Said Vanderberg; "and when we meet
 To-morrow, tell me I was right.   100

"Forget the dozen other things
 That you have not the faith to say;
For now I know as well as you
 That you are glad to go away."

I could have blessed the man for that,   105
 And he could read me with a smile:
"You doubt," said he, "but if we live
 You'll know me in a little while."

He lived; and all as he foretold,
 I knew him—better than he thought: 110
My fancy did not wholly dig
 The pit where I believed him caught.

But yet he lived and laughed, and preached,
  And worked—as only players can:
He scoured the shrine that once was home   115
  And kept himself a clergyman.

The clockwork of his cold routine
  Put friends far off that once were near;
The five staccatos in his laugh
  Were too defensive and too clear;   120

The glacial sermons that he preached
  Were longer than they should have been;
And, like the man who fashioned them,
  The best were too divinely thin.

But still he lived, and moved, and had   125
  The sort of being that was his,
Till on a day the shrine of home
  For him was in the Mysteries:—

"My friend, there's one thing yet," said he,
  "And one that I have never shared   130
With any man that I have met;
  But you—you know me." And he stared

For a slow moment at me then
  With conscious eyes that had the gleam,
The shine, before the stroke:—"You know   135
  The ways of us, the way we dream:

"You know the glory we have won,
  You know the glamour we have lost;
You see me now, you look at me,—
  And yes, you pity me, almost;   140

"But never mind the pity—no,
  Confess the faith you can't conceal;
And if you frown, be not like one
  Of those who frown before they feel.

"For there is truth, and half truth,—yes,   145
  And there's a quarter truth, no doubt;
But mine was more than half. . . . You smile?
  You understand? You bear me out?

"You always knew that I was right—
  You are my friend—and I have tried   150
Your faith—your love."—The gleam grew small,
  The stroke was easy, and he died.

I saw the dim look change itself
  To one that never will be dim;
I saw the dead flesh to the grave,   155
  But that was not the last of him.

For what was his to live lives yet:
  Truth, quarter truth, death cannot reach;
Nor is it always what we know
  That we are fittest here to teach.   160

The fight goes on when fields are still,
  The triumph clings when arms are down;
The jewels of all coronets
  Are pebbles of the unseen crown;

The specious weight of loud reproof   165
  Sinks where a still conviction floats;
And on God's ocean after storm
  Time's wreckage is half pilot-boats;

And what wet faces wash to sight
  Thereafter feed the common moan;— 170
But Vanderberg no pilot had,
  Nor could have: he was all alone.

Unchallenged by the larger light
  The starry quest was his to make;
And of all ways that are for men, 175
  The starry way was his to take.

We grant him idle names enough
  To-day, but even while we frown
The fight goes on, the triumph clings,
  And there is yet the unseen crown. 180

But was it his? Did Vanderberg
  Find half truth to be passion's thrall,
Or as we met him day by day,
  Was love triumphant, after all?

I do not know so much as that; 185
  I only know that he died right:
Saint Anthony nor Sainte-Nitouche
  Had ever smiled as he did—quite.

AS A WORLD WOULD HAVE IT

Alcestis

Shall I never make him look at me again?
I look at him, I look my life at him,
I tell him all I know the way to tell,
  But there he stays the same.

Shall I never make him speak one word to me?   5
Shall I never make him say enough to show
My heart if he be glad? Be glad? . . . ah! God,
    Why did they bring me back?

I wonder, if I go to him again,
If I take him by those two cold hands again,   10
Shall I get one look of him at last, or feel
    One sign—or anything?

Or will he still sit there in the same way,
Without an answer for me from his lips,
Or from his eyes,—or even with a touch   15
    Of his hand on my hand? . . .

"Will you look down this once—look down at me?
Speak once—and if you never speak again,
Tell me enough—tell me enough to make
    Me know that you are glad!   20

"You are my King, and once my King would speak:
You were Admetus once, you loved me once:
Life was a dream of heaven for us once—
    And has the dream gone by?

"Do I cling to shadows when I call you Life?   25
Do you love me still, or are the shadows all?
Or is it I that love you in the grave,
    And you that mourn for me?

"If it be that, then do not mourn for me;
Be glad that I have loved you, and be King.   30
But if it be not that—if it be true . . .
    Tell me if it be true!"

Then with a choking answer the King spoke;
But never touched his hand on hers, or fixed
His eyes on hers, or on the face of her: 35
    "Yes, it is true," he said.

"You are alive, and you are with me now;
And you are reaching up to me that I—
That I may take you—I that am a King—
    I that was once a man."   40

So then she knew. She might have known before;
Truly, she thought, she must have known it long
Before: she must have known it when she came
    From that great sleep of hers.

She knew the truth, but not yet all of it: 45
He loved her, but he would not let his eyes
Prove that he loved her; and he would not hold
    His wife there in his arms.

So, like a slave, she waited at his knees,
And waited. She was not unhappy now.   50
She quivered, but she knew that he would speak
    Again—and he did speak.

And while she felt the tremor of his words,
He told her all there was for him to tell;
And then he turned his face to meet her face,   55
    That she might look at him.

She looked; and all her trust was in that look,
And all her faith was in it, and her love;
And when his answer to that look came back,
    It flashed back through his tears.   60

So then she put her arms around his neck,
And kissed him on his forehead and his lips;
And there she clung, fast in his arms again,
    Triumphant, with closed eyes.

At last, half whispering, she spoke once more: 65
"Why was it that you suffered for so long?
Why could you not believe me—trust in me?
    Was I so strange as that?

"We suffer when we do not understand;
And you have suffered—you that love me now—   70
Because you are a man. . . . There is one thing
    No man can understand.

"I would have given everything?—gone down
To Tartarus—to silence? Was it that?
I would have died? I would have let you live?—   75
    And was it very strange?"

THE CORRIDOR

It may have been the pride in me for aught
I know, or just a patronizing whim;
But call it freak or fancy, or what not,
I cannot hide that hungry face of him.

I keep a scant half-dozen words he said,   5
And every now and then I lose his name;
He may be living or he may be dead,
But I must have him with me all the same.

I knew it, and I knew it all along,—
And felt it once or twice, or thought I did;   10
But only as a glad man feels a song
That sounds around a stranger's coffin lid.

I knew it, and he knew it, I believe,
But silence held us alien to the end;
And I have now no magic to retrieve   15
That year, to stop that hunger for a friend.

CORTÈGE

Four o'clock this afternoon,
Fifteen hundred miles away:
So it goes, the crazy tune,
So it pounds and hums all day.

Four o'clock this afternoon,   5
Earth will hide them far away:
Best they go to go so soon,
Best for them the grave to-day.

Had she gone but half so soon,
Half the world had passed away.   10
Four o'clock this afternoon,
Best for them they go to-day.

Four o'clock this afternoon
Love will hide them deep, they say;
Love that made the grave so soon,   15
Fifteen hundred miles away.

Four o'clock this afternoon—
Ah, but they go slow to-day:
Slow to suit my crazy tune,
Past the need of all we say.   20

Best it came to come so soon,
Best for them they go to-day:
Four o'clock this afternoon,
Fifteen hundred miles away.

THE WIFE OF PALISSY

Yes, you have it; I can see.
Beautiful? . . . Dear, look at me!
Look and let my shame confess
Triumph after weariness.
Beautiful? Ah, yes. 5

Lift it where the beams are bright;
Hold it where the western light,
Shining in above my bed,
Throws a glory on your head,
Now it is all said. 10

All there was for me to say
From the first until to-day.
Long denied and long deferred,
Now I say it in one word—
Now; and you have heard. 15

Life would have its way with us,
And I've called it glorious:
For I know the glory now
And I read it on your brow.
You have shown me how. 20

I can feel your cheeks all wet,
But your eyes will not forget:
In the frown you cannot hide
I can read where faith and pride
Are not satisfied. 25

But the word was, two should live:
Two should suffer—and forgive:
By the steep and weary way,
For the glory of the clay,
Two should have their day.   30

We have toiled and we have wept
For the gift the gods have kept:
Clashing and unreconciled
When we might as well have smiled,
We have played the child.   35

But the clashing is all past,
And the gift is yours at last.
Lift it—hold it high again! . . .
Did I doubt you now and then?
Well, we are not men.   40

Never mind; we know the way,—
And I do not need to stay.
Let us have it well confessed:
You to triumph, I to rest.
That will be the best.   45

TWILIGHT SONG

Through the shine, through the rain
We have shared the day's load;
To the old march again
We have tramped the long road;
We have laughed, we have cried,   5
And we've tossed the King's crown;
We have fought, we have died,
And we've trod the day down.

So it's lift the old song
Ere the night flies again,   10
Where the road leads along
Through the shine, through the rain.

Long ago, far away,
Came a sign from the skies;
And we feared then to pray   15
For the new sun to rise:
With the King there at hand,
Not a child stepped or stirred—
Where the light filled the land
And the light brought the word;   20
For we knew then the gleam
Though we feared then the day,
And the dawn smote the dream
Long ago, far away.

But the road leads us all,   25
For the King now is dead;
And we know, stand or fall,
We have shared the day's bread.
We can laugh down the dream,
For the dream breaks and flies;   30
And we trust now the gleam,
For the gleam never dies;—
So it's off now the load,
For we know the night's call,
And we know now the road   35
And the road leads us all.

Through the shine, through the rain,
We have wrought the day's quest;
To the old march again
We have earned the day's rest;   40
We have laughed, we have cried,

And we've heard the King's groans;
We have fought, we have died,
And we've burned the King's bones,
And we lift the old song   45
Ere the night flies again,
Where the road leads along
Through the shine, through the rain.

❦ ❦ ❦

Letters

TO HARRY DE FOREST SMITH

Gardiner
February 8, 1891

. . . Speaking of novels makes me think of one I have just read. For some time I have been intending to try something of Thomas Hardy's but never came to until a few days ago, when I borrowed *The Mayor of Casterbridge*. It was a revelation to me. I never would suppose that a writer of such power could achieve so little popularity (in the general sense of the word) as he has done. The book in question is a novel of something less than three hundred pages, but when you come to "finis" you have the impression of having read a whole history—the history of a quiet pastoral neighborhood which leaves in your mind the odor of an enviable rusticity. (Perhaps "odor" is hardly the word to use here, but you may supply what you will). In the main, the book is loaded with a certain drowsy elegance which tends to make the reader a little sleepy; but it is never tedious, as there is enough incident to keep one well on the lookout for the story as well as the wonderful style in which it is written. At times it is disastrously pathetic; and I am perfectly willing to confess that my *fons lachrymarum* was tapped once or twice to a troublesome extent during my perusal of it. I do not mean that the brine took the stiffening out of my collar, but that a certain unpleasant haze clouded my sight, ...

TO HARRY DE FOREST SMITH

Gardiner
March 10, 1891

. . . I am reading Carlyle's *Sartor Resartus* and am completely soaked with its fiery philosophy. It is just the book for you to read, as, in the midst of your philosophical and psychological moonings you will find it a most welcome guest. There is a certain half-diabolical humor running through that renders it all the more readable. The general tone is cynical, but never morbid. . . . I am willing to confess that there are many passages that I entirely fail to understand; but in the main it is intelligible and entertaining, —instructive, and I think upon the whole, elevating. The introduction states that he had a most doleful experience in finding a publisher; this seems to be the case with nearly all great literary efforts.

There is an article in the last *Arena* by Albert Ross, entitled "What is Immoral in Literature?" I have not read it but probably you have. It seems to me that, from a commonsense standpoint, there can be no possible defense for that gentleman's fiction (or perhaps we had better say, truth). It is the simplest thing in the world for a person with the gift of writing to concoct a slimy tale after the fashion of *Sapho, The Pace that Kills, Thou Shalt Not,* etc. and conclude it with what it pleases the author to call a moral, but so doing does not detract from the book's filthiness or pernicious influence. The first two books named above do not make the rather ghastly moral pretensions of the latter, but I consider them quite as [un]pardonable. Do not think that I am setting myself up for a Saint Anthony (Comstock) for I am not; but I will say that the recent deluge of literary nastiness that has poured for the past two or three years from the soul-sewers of six or eight half-penny writers without any special literary excellence to aid them in their obviously mercenary mission has been a disgrace to American letters. Neither Ross nor Saltus are literary artists, and their books are only bought by an itching gullible public whose mind is too shallow to realize its shallowness. Perhaps, though, I am a little too hard with Saltus, for some of his essays are said to be, in a way, fine. . . .

TO HARRY DE FOREST SMITH

Gardiner
May 21, 1891

. . . I think I told you that I would copy off the ode of Horace, and I will do so upon another sheet. You will find it rather too literal for a poetical translation—a little prosy in places. I have not tried Horace since and I doubt if I ever do again. It is too much work for the pay. I have never seen an English translation of Horace that seemed satisfactory to me; perhaps I am over particular, but I doubt if the thing can be done to catch the spirit of the original. Horace is Latin, or nothing. For example, make a poetical translation of *"cras ingens iterabimus aequor,"* or *"Integer vitae, scelerisque purus."* Bulwer says, "Tomorrow again the great sea-plains," but it sounds rather far-fetched to me. His translation of the odes and epodes is a rather unique one, however, and it would pay you to examine it if you have never done so. He attempts to reproduce the ring of the different metres in different styles of English blank verse, mostly of his own invention I should say. If I remember rightly he renders *"dulce loquentem"*—"her the sweet-talking"—objective of course.

Well, I think I shall have to paddle down street through the rain after a plug of tobacco and have a smoke. I will copy that ode and take this letter along with me.

Please excuse the dimness of the type: there is evidently a scarcity of ink.

Horace: Book I., Ode XI.

I pray thee not, Leuconoe, to pore
    Upon forbidden things—what end may be
    By destiny allowed for you and me—
Nor blind Chaldea's starry page explore.

'Twere better, oh! far better, if you bore
　　Your lot contented: whether Jove decree
More winters yet to come, or whether he
Assign this one whose worn, wave-eaten shore
Shatters the Tyrian sea to-day the last—
　　Be wise, I pray; and rack thy wine, nor fill
　　　　Thy bosom with large hopes; for while I sing
　　　　The envious close of time is narrowing:
So seize the day, be merry ere 'tis past,
　　And let the morrow come for what it will.

　　　　　　　　　　　　　　　　　　E. A. R.

TO HARRY DE FOREST SMITH

Gardiner
September 13, 1891

. . . I shall have a change soon, however, as my application to Harvard has been accepted and I shall probably leave Gardiner about the 27th. I expect it will seem rather odd at first, but I trust I shall get used to the new life in a few weeks. As I am not subject to "swelled head" and have no idea of overturning the faculty, I see no reason why I should not be an "eddy of the mighty stream" and pass with the multitude. His erudition, M. Frédéric César de Sumichrast will be my adviser, and I shall be obliged to hold a parly with him before I enter upon my course. Entering as a special student is far from satisfactory, but it is better than nothing. It will give me a taste of the college atmosphere and cause me to mingle with people of all sorts and conditions—a thing which I sadly need. The truth is, I have lived in Gardiner for nearly twenty-two years and, metaphorically speaking, hardly been out of the yard. Now this is not right; the process tends to widen one's thoughts, or rather sympathies, to an unwholesome extent. This may be a new theory, but I firmly believe it to be the truth. Solitude (in the broad sense of the word) tends to magnify one's ideas of individuality; it sharpens his sympathy for failure where fate has been abused and self demoralized; it renders a man suspicious of the whole natural plan, and leads him to wonder whether the invisible powers are a fortuitous issue of unguided cosmos, or the cosmos itself—"The master of the show," as Omar Khayyam says. In short, this living alone is bad business; and I have had more than my share of it.

But here the old question comes up again, Why have I not done differently? I cannot conscientiously say that it has been necessary that I should stay at home as I have; and the more I think it over, the more am I convinced that the fault lies with myself. But how about the unseen powers? The old buffers (no offence to them) will smoke their pipes and cut their coupons and tell us all about how the world is what we make it, and how every man is the architect of his own fortune, etc. It is good to hear them, but I sometimes have a clambering idea that perhaps there is another architect behind ourselves. This is probably moral cowardice, and the chances are, ten to one, that the element is but an outgrowth of objective inactivity. . . .

TO HARRY DE FOREST SMITH

717 Cambridge St.
Cambridge, Mass.
December 8, 1891

. . . Then came a knock at the door; and at my yell of "Come!" in stepped Robert Morss Eliott, perhaps the leading spirit of Harvard outside of athletics. Of course Capt. Trafford and his crew are with the immortals. Eliott is a Senior and in many respects a remarkable man. Without any "gushing," I actually felt honored to receive a call from him, being a Special and a first year man at that. He is editor in chief of the *Monthly* and brought back the manuscript of my sonnet on Thomas Hood. At a meet-

ing of the board of editors it was weighed in the balance and
found wanting. (Perhaps I have some foolish opinions of my
own, but they are of no value in this case). We talked of college
papers and kindred matters for about half an hour, when he left
with a request for another contribution—which I have decided to
make—and an urgent request to call on him. If I succeed in getting in with such fellows as that, college life will prove most
agreeable. I think the best way to do it will be to keep silence on
the matter of contributions. I may change my mind but these
are my feelings at present. I was sailing along in such elegant
shape, putting whatever I chose into the *Advocate*, that I must
confess this declination put a slight "damper" on me; but Mr.
Lovett (I wrote Eliott before by mistake—must have been thinking of the President)—showed himself to be such a gentleman
and "white man" that I could not feel offended. If I am a little
foxy I may get in with the whole gang, which will be rather
more pleasant than my present situation. Of course I have found
some good fellows—but you will understand precisely what I
mean. I will send you the *Advocate* with Villanelle tomorrow
with this letter. Perhaps I have tired you with talk of my own
affairs, but you know that I am prone to enter into confidence
with now and then a fellow spirit [*sic*]. Of course I need not ask
you not to mention anything that I have written. . . .

TO HARRY DE FOREST SMITH

1691 Cambridge St.
Cambridge, Mass.
April 17, 1892

. . . I have been loafing around my room all day and cannot
seem to get over chronic Sunday laziness. I have longed for most
everything that I cannot have, including that patch of woods
behind your house in Gardiner, and the pipes. I had my own
pipe, to be sure, but it tasted lonesome. I have an idea that that

is figurative language, but I did not intend any poetry. I do not feel like it. I have made a little verse today, however—part of a sonnet beginning:

> "I make no measure of the words they say
>   Who come with snaky tongues to me and tell
>   Of all the woe awaiting me in Hell
> When from this goodly world I go my way, etc."

Eventually I shall go on to say how the appearance of a good wholesome white-haired man who never told a lie or drank Maine whiskey impresses me, and how I draw a lesson from the unspoken sermon of his own self and begin to realize the real magnificence of better things—the which I have an idea will make the closing line. I shall spring it on the *Advocate.* They may object to the morality of it, though, and throw it out. If they do I have another for them beginning:

> "There is a drear and lonely tract of Hell
>   From all the common woe removed afar,—
>   A flat sad land where only shadows are
> Whose lorn estate no word of mine can tell, etc."

I don't know how long this Hell business will last, but I may sigh out two or three more. It is a damned cheerful subject and my muse is merry whenever she gets into it. Sometimes I think that Hell may not be such a bad place after all. If there is brimstone, it may be a little unpleasant, but otherwise I do not think a man need be afraid of it. Think of the company he will have. Who knows but you and I may sit upon a red-hot boulder and read Daudet and Zola? That would not be so bad after we got used to the caloric. . . .

TO HARRY DE FOREST SMITH

1691 Cambridge St.
Cambridge, Mass.
May 23, 1892

At last I have settled myself and will try to write you a letter. Yesterday I could not get a chance. Since 7:30 this evening I have attended a lecture on *Sir Gawain and the Green Knight* by Prof. Kittredge, read some of *Middlemarch* and smoked a pipe. The lecture was peculiarly interesting—much more so than the subject would lead one to think. He first read a translation (his own) of the more prominent portions of the poem and concluded with comments, historical and critical. In his translation he endeavored to keep the tone and flavor of the original as far as possible and, as far as I am able to judge, succeeded admirably. If you have ever read any of *Piers Plowman* you can have some idea of the alliterative swing of the story. It is supposed to have been written somewhere in the latter half of the fourteenth century, but the author is unknown.

There was something fascinating in the Prof's version of it. He clung to Saxon words almost exclusively and some of the lines were, to say the least, unique. Here is one in particular that I remember: " 'Twas the cursedest kirk he ever had entered." The only unsatisfactory feature of the affair was the small audience. Sever 11 seats about five hundred people and I should not think there could have been over fifty or sixty there at the most.

As to *Middlemarch,* I regret to say that I am unable to appreciate the transcendent beauties of Geo. Eliot's character analysis. To me, she makes more of human character than life itself warrants. Thackeray is to me the ideal student of human nature. To be sure, his creatures are to some extent types but not in the sense that those of Dickens are. Dickens deals almost exclusively in exaggerated characteristics; Thackeray with definitely drawn and coherent characters; while Geo. Eliot's works are a study of formative influences and psychological results. In my opinion she stands below Jane Austen though she deals less with complex destiny. I may reveal my uneducated taste in making this confession of my opinions, but a fellow may as well tell the truth. . . .

TO HARRY DE FOREST SMITH

1716 Cambridge St.
Cambridge, Mass.
November 29, 1892

. . . The worst thing I have is French Comp. I wish you could hear one of Prof. Norton's lectures in "Fine Arts." They are simply magnificent. Today he said that there was not half as much buncombe in the Darius Inscription which May [sic, Henry?] Rawlinson spent ten years in copying from a cliff in some god-forsaken region in Mesopotamia as there is in one of Chauncey Depew's after-dinner speeches. He likes to swipe the World's Fair and enjoys telling the anecdote of the Chicago man who said "they had not much culture out there yet, but when they got it, they were going to make it hum." You know John Ruskin calls Norton "his first tutor." I suppose there is no doubt that he is by all odds the greatest man in America, and I am beginning to realize what a privilege it is to sit within six feet of him three times a week and hear him talk. . . .

TO HARRY DE FOREST SMITH

1716 Cambridge St.
Cambridge, Mass.
February 5, 1893

Now I will try to write you a letter, though I am feeling about as miserably as a mortal can, and be religious. I have had a tremendous pain in my left lung for the past two or three days and now I am "broken out" in big blotches both fore and aft. I have no idea what it is, but will consult an M.D. tomorrow. I always prided myself on my strong lungs, and if there is anything the matter with them I shall feel rather down in the mouth. I hate to kick, but it seems as if the Fates kept something in store for me all the time to keep me in hot water. After that long siege with my ear which no one can appreciate but myself, this thing comes on like a cannibal after a missionary. It may be a cancer or a lupus; if it is, I shall dodge the exams. in English VII and Philosophy (Logic and Psychology) on general principles, and so gain something. Last night the thing acted so that I went down to the square and got a porous plaster, which I fancy relieved it somewhat. In order to drive the pain away I read Emerson's essays on "Love," "Friendship," "Prudence," and "Heroism," but am afraid I did not get much out of them. . . .

TO HARRY DE FOREST SMITH

Cambridge
June 11, 1893

. . . I have two more examinations yet to take, French and English, and then my Harvard career will be at an end. I have no particular desire to come another year, but I would hate to part with the experience of the past two. I have lived, upon the whole, a very quiet life, but for all that I have seen things that I could not possibly see at any other place, and have a different conception of what is good and bad in life. From the standpoint of marks, my course here has been a failure, as I knew well enough it would be; but that is the last thing in the world I came here for. Grinding for marks does not command my admiration except in case of pecuniary necessity. Under those conditions, it often borders on the heroic. You have no idea of what some men go through here, unless that little book on "Students' Expenses" worked upon your imagination to a considerable extent. . . .

TO HARRY DE FOREST SMITH

Gardiner
October 1, 1893

You are probably getting a little impatient by this time, but I have made a "big brace" at last and am going to write you a letter, or something that will take the place of one. My room is too cold for a free flow of thought, and I may get discouraged at the end of the first page; but my inclinations are all right, and with a little effort of imagination you will be able to fill in as many more pages as you like.

I have nothing in particular to say except that it is rather lonesome here without you, and on dark, dull Sundays like this I find it [hard] to be cheerful and optimistic, and everything else that a useful man should be in order to fill his place in nature to the satisfaction of himself and his dear friends who feel so much for his welfare. I am half afraid that my "dear friends" here in Gardiner will be disappointed in me if I do not do something before long, but somehow I don't care half as much about the matter as I ought. One of my greatest misfortunes is the total inability to admire the so called successful men who are pointed out to poor devils like me as examples for me to follow and revere. If Merchant A and Barrister B are put here as "ensamples to mortals," I am afraid that I shall always stand in the shadow as one of Omar's broken pots. I suspect that I am pretty much what I am, and that I am pretty much a damned fool in many ways; but I further suspect that I am not altogether an ass, whatever my neighbors may say. I may live to see this egotistic idea exploded, but until that time comes I am to hug my own particular phantoms and think as I like. . . .

TO HARRY DE FOREST SMITH

Gardiner
January 27, 1894

. . . Yesterday I finished my sketch—the revision—called "Three Merry Gentlemen and their Wives." It is not a particularly cheerful thing but I cannot help having some faith in it. Tomorrow I shall commence a sketch which I have some fear of never bringing out to anything like satisfaction on my part. It deals with the selfishness of self-denial—a peculiar but by no means rare flaw of human nature, but perhaps a little beyond my poor abilities. I shall have the thing done by next Sunday, and can tell you more about it then. I am beginning to realize my artistic deficiencies, and can look ahead without many qualms to a hard apprenticeship. As it is, it takes me about a week to get out the first draft of a four thousand word sketch—so you see I do some work. Four hours a day is my limit at present, after that my head spins.

Yesterday afternoon I began to read Coppée's *Toute une Jeunesse*—a personal narrative modeled after *David Copperfield*. It begins magnificently and I look forward to much enjoyment from its pages—a little over 300. The book is published in English under the title of *Disillusions*. I am already much interested in the schoolmaster with the geographical cranium, and the artist with the Abd-el-Kadir pipe. . . .

TO HARRY DE FOREST SMITH

Gardiner
February 4, 1894

I find that I misjudged things in telling you that I should have my study of "the selfishness of self-denial" finished by today. The fact is it is only a little over half done, but I think I see my way out of it. I have to put a good deal in a few words and there is a great danger of a general effect of "roughness." When the thing is smoothed out and copied it will be the best piece of work I have done yet, which, I suppose, is not saying a great deal. It is "No. 4" in my recent ambitious series, and, as I said in my last, a little too complex for a short sketch in the hands of a novice. I am anxious to read it to you and get your candid opinion of its merits or faults, as the case may be. My next work will be in a lighter vein—the sketch of a philosophical tramp ("Anxious Hendricks," probably) looking for rest. Merely an experiment in a new field.—Forgive me for saying so much about myself in this and my past letters, but you see what a hold the scheme has upon me. If it fails totally, I think I shall get drunk and then hunt for a "job." "Let the dream go!" says the poet. Good advice, perhaps, but like all good advice, hard to follow.

I have only worked five or six hours during the past week. I had an itch for reading and tired my eyes in consequence. I finished *Toute une Jeunesse* by Coppée and did a lot of browsing through various books of poems and essays. Tomorrow I hope to settle down in earnest and bring something to pass before next Sunday. When the five sketches are all finished up to the best of my ability, I intend to copy them on the machine, and start them somewhere. The expectation of a returned manuscript is better than no excitement at all.

I have [been] thinking up a little scheme for this summer, but shall make no promises, even if it is agreeable to you. I think you first suggested something of the kind. My scheme is to make a metrical translation of the *Antigone*. You might find pleasure and profit in writing out a correct prose version of the play, keeping the Greek spirit as much as possible, and in guiding me in the choice of words and suggestions as to the classical effect of my verses. My choice would be to make it in the main unrhymed, depending upon sonority and picturesqueness for the effect. If the thing should prove anything like a success we might have a small edition printed at the cost of an ordinary indulgence in the world's pleasures. A title page something like this would not be bad:

> "The Antigone of Sophocles: A translation by Harry de Forest Smith and Edwin Arlington Robinson.—An edition of fifty copies printed for private circulation. Gardiner, Maine. REPORTER-JOURNAL JOB PRESS (!) MDCCCXCIV."

This will probably end up like the stone house on the hill, but we have a right to build castles in Spain or where we please. This is a kind of Spanish castle in Greece. I wonder if the shade of Sophocles is grinning over my shoulder as I write this? If he is, I suppose he knows how the thing is coming out. The one great objection to this performance is the time it would take. The question is, would the time be well spent? Somehow all my schemes involve the spending of money instead of the making of it. If time is money, I make way with a fortune every week. I suppose I shall keep on doing this and live from hand to mouth all the days of my life. Sometimes the realization of my non-success thus far in my life make me totally discouraged for days at a time. Then it clears away and I am full of hope again. The things that I enjoy the most—no matter how much labor they may require are the things that keep me from getting on in the world, as the practical men say. You, who are making a living, cannot imagine how cutting it is for a man of twenty-four to depend upon his mother for every cent he has and every mouthful he swallows. But I won't dwell longer upon this,—I begin to hear the dog in the manger. . . .

TO HARRY DE FOREST SMITH

Gardiner
February 25, 1894

. . . The past week has been a rather dull one for me and pretty much wasted. I have not been able to do much of any work, for some reason I cannot explain. I have felt well enough bodily but I have been in a bad mood. Yesterday I partially drove it off by making a rondeau and a villanelle. The latter is a little mystical perhaps and is an attempt to show the poetry of the commonplace. Here it is,—you may judge for yourself. Tell me what you think of it and do not be afraid of hurting my feelings.

The House on the Hill.
(Villanelle of Departure.)

They are all gone away,
 The house is shut and still:
There is nothing more to say.

Malign them as we may,
 We cannot do them ill:
They are all gone away.

Are we more fit than they
 To meet the Master's will?—
There is nothing more to say.

What matters it who stray
 Around the sunken sill?—
They are all gone away,

And our poor fancy-play
 For them is wasted skill:
There is nothing more to say.

> There is ruin and decay
> > In the House on the Hill:
> They are all gone away,
> There is nothing more to say. . . .

This kind of thing may not interest you much, and please do not hesitate to say so if that be the case. These old French forms always had a fascination for me which I never expect to outgrow. I don't know that I care to outgrow it, but still it interferes with my more serious work to an unpleasant extent. When one of the things begin to run in my mind there is little rest for me until it is out. Fortunately this one was made very quickly (in about twenty minutes) so did not steal much of my time.

I have been thinking a good deal lately about the *Antigone* scheme. I like it and would like to carry it out; but I am half afraid that the double load of that and my prose work will [be] a little too much. On the other hand, the time and trouble might be a good investment for the practice it would give me in the choice and arrangement of words. Perhaps we had better try it and see how fast we progress. I could hardly hope to arrange more than ten lines a day. At that rate the thing would be done in about a year if I have a correct idea of the length of the drama. Isn't it something like three thousand lines? I should want a good translation to thoroughly familiarize myself with the work and then you could send me your version—a little at a time. At this rate we ought to do a thousand lines during your vacation, which would be a good start. I am inclined to think, upon the whole, that the time would be well spent, though as I am now situated it is a question of conscience rather than labor. When I have one definite idea to work out, have I a moral right to let such a laborious amusement interfere with it? That is the trouble. It is a little different with you, as you are making a living and have the summer to improve as best you may. I know something about the labor involved in a task of this kind from my past experience in translating Virgil and an ode from Horace. In the "days of my youth," about eight years ago, I put the whole of Cicero's first oration against Catiline into blank verse. I began it for fun and carried it through to save myself the chagrin of giving the thing [up]. Sometimes I am afraid it would be the same with *Antigone,* though of course I should go into this work with much more earnestness. I have a presentiment that the thing will be done, and that we shall be vastly glad that we have done it. It is no small undertaking, and must reflect some credit upon the men who carry it through—even though it be a questionable success. In years to come we could look back upon the business and feel that we had left the common ways of men and at least striven for higher things. When the thing is completed (if it ever is) it would be a good plan for you to submit it to some Brunswick man whom you think well qualified to test its merits from all points of view—that is, if you are upon sufficiently familiar terms with any of them to warrant your asking so much. If it were good for anything it would be folly not to preserve it in print. I should prefer to do the metrical work without having seen any poetical translations whatever. Then I could feel that I was not imitating. I should want a Greek text to follow the form of the lines (a knowledge of the alphabet would be enough for that) and I think it would be a good plan for you to bring the books you mentioned in your letter. I do not mean that I intend to attempt anything like a reproduction of the Greek metres— my idea is merely to suggest a little of the original form to the American eye—thus preserving an ocular resemblance between the translation and the Greek text. . . .

TO HARRY DE FOREST SMITH

Gardiner
March 18, 1894

I worked my way over the hills to your house the other day, and brought back a satchel full of books on the Greek drama. I think I have managed to get a fairly good idea of the general scheme of *Antigone,* though I cannot help thinking that there is a book in existence that would tell me many things I do not know. I have about concluded to write the body of the play in regular English heroic verse, making up a kind of irregular ode for the chorus—I mean irregular in meter but to correspond in the antistrophes, thus making the thing balance and showing up a definite plan on my part. I have this in mind for an opening:

$$\acute{} \,/\, \breve{}\,\acute{} \,/\, \breve{}\,\acute{} \,//\, \acute{} \,/\, \breve{}\,\acute{} \,/\, \breve{}\,\acute{} \,/\, \breve{}\,\acute{}$$

$$\acute{} \,/\, \breve{}\,\acute{} \,/\, \breve{}\,\acute{} \,/\, \breve{} \,//\, \acute{} \,/\, \breve{}\,\acute{} \,/\, \breve{}\,\acute{}$$

This, as you see, is very simple, but not too much so, if I can keep up a sufficient sonority. I cannot recall anything just like it in English poetry, but it must have been used before now. If I remember rightly, the envoi in *Many Inventions* is very near to it, though I think it is slightly different.

I am afraid I have undertaken a task beyond my abilities, but there will be some satisfaction in an honest attempt. If I fail, the trial must be worth something for the experience it will give me. I have been thinking the matter over during the past week and wondering whether the project is asinine or not. To be sure, Bryant translated the *Iliad* and *Odyssey* without being a Greek scholar, but regular hexameter verse is marvelously different from the split metres of the drama. I am just mutton-headed enough to carry this thing out, if I can, without looking into any English poetical translation. If I make the ghost of Sophocles shudder, I cannot help it. Sometimes I am foolish enough to believe that my ignorance of Greek (I think I have said this before) may be a benefit rather than a hindrance. I know that I have something of the Hellenic spirit in me, and have a pretty good conception of what the word means. I may lack some of the "serene and childlike joy of life" but I have the spirit of wise moderation and love of classical completeness which, I suppose, is more marked in the later poets of Pericles' time than in the Homeric period. This will help me amazingly in *Antigone*. You have much of this appreciation and I shall depend to a large extent upon your judgment as to the choice of words.—Do not think by this everlasting talk of my own part of the business that I overlook your own part of the work; for you know you must give me something more than an ordinary slipshod class-room rendering. You must weigh your words and keep the original spirit in the prose version which I must try to intensify in my verses. In short, you must do your best to make your prose version a work of art. The result will probably be that your rendering will prove more satisfying than mine—provided you do your work as conscientiously as you do almost everything you enter upon.

Today I shall finish the revision of my "Parable of the Pines." The scheme is pretty good and I really think that the thing might be of some benefit to the world, on account of its subject matter alone, if it once got circulated. This is my seventh and last sketch for the time being. My work for the next two or three weeks will be the general polishing up and final copying of what I have done—preparatory to sending it away. I want your opinions very much, and shall probably tire you a little with my questions. But you know that I would be willing to do the same for you if the chance was offered, so you may be able to wake a little enthusiasm in the matter. All of my last six pieces are entirely different from "Marshall," but I am beginning to doubt if they are any better.—Yesterday the idea of a very simple and appropriate book-plate came into my mind and I proceeded to draw the rough sketch I enclose. It hardly seems possible that it can be original, but I do not think I have ever seen it.

TO HARRY DE FOREST SMITH

Gardiner
April 22, 1894

. . . Excepting *The Task*, I have read little during the past week. I wonder why it is that I like Cowper as I do? Something tells me that he is not, and never will be, one of the really great poets, although in occasional passages he is well nigh unsurpassable. There is much of the sandy desert in his work, but still it is comfortable travelling. The green and glorious places that come every little while are all the brighter for the comparative barrenness around them. His religion is akin to mawkish to a man of my doubts, but I readily overlook that in the consideration of his temperament and his surroundings. He is popularly and justly, I suppose, called feminine; but human nature has a word to say regarding such matters, and a little sympathy is not likely to be wasted upon this poet. His timidity was a disease, and the making of verse and rabbit-hutches, together with gardening, was his occupation. He was a strange man; and this strangeness, with his almost pathetic sincerity, go to make up the reason for my fondness for his poetry. He stands between Thomson and Wordsworth, and for some reason, he seems to stand on pretty firm ground. I do not think another half-century will disturb him to any great extent. His description of the wood-cutter and his dog cannot die while men and women care for true art in homely things.

I have written a queer poem, but I haven't the nerve to send it to you yet. It needs a little revision before [being] subjected to even the most friendly criticism, and it is in this little revision that my difficulty lies. The whole thing—forty lines—was written between twelve and one o'clock while I was waiting for my dinner, and has an air of unsatisfactory completeness about it which I

am at a loss to overcome. When I fix it, I shall send you a copy
—yes I will send you two stanzas now while I am talking about
it:

> Yes, this is the end of life, I suppose—
>   To do what we can for ourselves and others;
> But men who find tragedy writ in a rose
>   May forget sometimes there are sons and mothers—
>
> Fathers and daughters of love and hate,
>   Scattered like hell-spawn down from Heaven,
> To teach mankind to struggle and wait
>   Till life be over and death forgiven.

I call the thing "Doubts." The stanzas quoted are the fifth and
sixth out of ten. I think that there is at least a straightforward-
ness—what a devil of a word that is!—about the poem, which
you will like. There is nothing artificial, and, I fear, little intelligible; but for all that I rather think you will like it better than
the "House on the Hill." As for myself, I think I prefer the
villanelle. I have a weakness for the suggestiveness of those artificial forms—that is, when they treat of something besides bride-
roses and ball-rooms. *Vers de société* pure and simple, has little
charm for me. Austin Dobson might be twice the man he is if he
were—somebody else, I suppose; but it does seem that he might
have used his talents to a little better advantage. "Don Quixote"
shows what is in him; if it could be let out, England would be
the richer by another poet.

TO HARRY DE FOREST SMITH

Gardiner
May 20, 1894

. . . Yes, I am glad you are going to be married. I have always looked upon a bachelor as only half of a man, though this is of course too violent language to use. I have always believed in love, and always shall believe in it. The fact that so many thousands go astray sometimes shakes my faith a little, but it always rights itself after a time. There are natures that positively cannot be faithful to a single companion, and sometimes the people who have them seem to be the happiest in the world; but I think if we knew them as well as they know themselves (I use "know" in its everyday sense) we should find there is something in their souls that is never satisfied,—their lives are not complete, they live without a mission. Their life is a fevered irregularity, and, when they are past their forties—and oftentimes long before that —the original nature stamps itself in the face, and those lines of hardness which we have all seen, tell us that something is wrong. . . .

"L'Amour" is pitifully abused in spoken and written literature. The word is used without a particle of consideration as to its better meaning. Love and lust have become so mixed by our poets and novelists that we poor puritans are half inclined to wonder, as we read, whether there is such a thing after all, as a better nature in man or woman. The modern French school is doing its best to kill these higher sensibilities, and their work is not wholly a failure in that direction. It may sound foolish, but I know it to be a fact that many fellows who ought to know better are mentally and morally debilitated by the matchless trash produced by such writers as Maupassant, Mendès and Gautier. I can stand a good deal in the way of freedom of expression, but I am disgusted with many of our modern tendencies. I make these few remarks on love because I am glad to know that there are still men in these progressive days of ours who can value it for its true worth. When you get to read Shakspere (you are bound to do so someday) you will find in all his later plays an undertone of manly melancholy which you will naturally trace to a love of the higher kind, which, for some unknown reason, was never satisfied. . . .

TO HARRY DE FOREST SMITH

Gardiner
May 27, 1894

. . . I have been too much occupied of late to do any writing except two sonnets and some ninety lines of a queer poem called "The Night Before." I hope to have it done (there will be some four hundred lines of it) by the time you return and I think you may like it. It is a tragic monologue written in unrhymed tetrameters—that is, like *Evangeline*, with two feet left out. For example, here is the opening line:

"Look you, Domine; look you, and listen."

Yesterday I did fifty-five lines, but was pretty tired after it was over. You see the thing demands work—wasted work, most likely, but still work that I cannot seem to help doing. You will be glad, or sorry, to know that I have three prose tales well in my head and shall have them out as soon as I can settle myself down to such labor once more. The one I like best of all cannot fail to attract you, even when done in my poor way; but the title, "Theodore," you won't like. It seems to me, however, the only title for the story, which, by the way, is not just like most stories, and I could not think of changing it. . . .

TO HARRY DE FOREST SMITH

Gardiner
June 3, 1894

. . . I have written 225 lines of "The Night Before," and am getting rather enthusiastic over the thing. The story is pretty good and the writing of it is the most difficult thing that I have ever undertaken. These two facts serve as incentives. Fifteen lines an hour is good work and I feel much better after I have done them. The story is unpleasant, founded upon my system of "opposites" that is, creating a fictitious life in direct opposition to a real life which I know. My recent mental disturbances have rendered some kind of more or less literary expression an absolute necessity; and this story, which by the way, comes dangerously near to being what the world calls "hot stuff" is doing me a good service in working off my general discontent. It reflects, in a measure, my present mood in the narration of things of which I know nothing except by instinctive fancy. There is battle (of the worst kind), murder and sudden death in it, together with other things equally interesting were they put in the hands of a competent writer. As it is, I think you may enjoy it, but I must ask you not to expect too much, and to make a strong effort not to laugh at the attempted intensity of my murderer's confession. The success of the poem will depend wholly upon the success of this intensity, which ought to increase from the start and end with a grand smash. At any rate, you will think well of me for trying to do something a little above the ordinary, whether I succeed or not. Here is a little observation that will come in towards the end:

> "I tell you, Domine,
> There are times in the lives of us poor devils
> When heaven and hell get mixed."

The main purpose of the thing is to show that men and women are individuals; and there is a minor injunction running through it not to thump a man too hard when he is down. This, however, is hidden, and would probably not be noticed by one reader in a hundred. If the poem is a little fatalistic, you must excuse me. I write it because I cannot help it, and this is also true of the way in which I do it. . . .

TO HARRY DE FOREST SMITH

Gardiner
February 3, 1895

I had not quite finished *The Manxman* when I wrote last Sunday, so could not give you my final impressions. If you care for them now, I will say that the author proves his greatness by making the book a success in spite of its fearful length. Scene after scene is spoiled by over preparation and half the book is worse than padding. Still it is a great work and Caine is a great man.

In turning from *The Manxman* to *The Blithedale Romance* the contrast is bewildering. How did Hawthorne do it? That is the question that bothers me and I have come to the conclusion that much of it is due to the fact that he was capable of an amount of brain racking and tinkering of which the modern ink-spiller has no conception. The fact that the writing of *The Marble Faun* was a five years' job is enough to make a man stop and think. I do not think that I ever fully realized the greatness of Hawthorne until I took up the novel I bought of you. (Did I ever pay you for it?) Not that it is the best, but it somehow reveals the master in a way that is not to be noted in the others. There is a sense of reality about it which is utterly wanting in *The Scarlet Letter*; and there is a kind of glorification of little things which only a great master is likely to find worth while.

When I leave Hawthorne for my own poor, patient manuscript I feel very foolish indeed; but I get over that and go pegging away—sometimes a page at a time without any trouble—sometimes spending an hour over a dozen words. . . .

TO HARRY DE FOREST SMITH

Gardiner
May 12, 1895

I have been reading the *New Testament* (Matthew and Mark, which are pretty much alike) and am just beginning to realize what the rising generation is losing by letting such reading go by. For we all know well enough that the "scriptures" are the last thing that a fellow takes up nowadays, though it comes natural, for some reason, for a girl to know all about them. I have found that I can satisfy myself very well with the Big Book and I doubt if I read much else this summer save that and some French novels. The combination may point to certain paganistic tendencies on my part, but is far better to read the *Bible* as mere literature than to read most of the stuff that is printed in these days for anything at all. . . .

TO HARRY DE FOREST SMITH

Gardiner
December 14, 1895

. . . The poetry-book is getting on and will be pretty well shaken out by the first of February—sent off, I hope. When that comes back I shall be stirred up for a few days, but not for many. It isn't worth while. And on the other hand it isn't half so easy to put such things out of one's mind as it may seem to you who have never had the experience—as far as I know. You may be a *literatus,* "on the quiet," but I don't believe it. You have more respect for your brains. . . .

I have been rebuilding that sonnet translation of Horace's ode to Leuconoë. How do you like these for the opening lines?—

> "I pray you not, Leuconoë, to pore
> With unpermitted eyes on what may be
> Appointed by the gods for you and me,
> Nor on Chaldean figures any more."

I may get the thing to partly satisfy me some day, but I rather doubt it. I have spent the last three weeks mostly in rewriting that story of mine, "The Night Before"—you may remember it —in blank verse. "Look you Domine, look you and listen etc." I don't know what it all amounts to, but there are some pretty good passages in it and they may lug it through. My songs are corkers—particularly Edward Alphabet:

> "Look at Edward Alphabet
> Going home to pray!
> Drunk as he can ever get,
> And on the Sabbath day!—"

and so forth. You may not think it from the first lines but the poem is an argument against the present attitude of the females. I also have a piece of deliberate degeneration called "Luke Havergal," which is not at all funny. Then there is old John Everel-down who had all the women of Tilbury Town under his wing, or thought he had. The "Tavern" part of my book is not like anything I ever wrote before and I doubt much if I ever try anything like it again. The songs have been for the most part villainously hard to make. . . .

TO HARRY DE FOREST SMITH

Gardiner
March 7, 1896

. . . If the book should make its way then, my satisfaction would be proportionally greater. I am sure of one thing, however, and that is that they are to be printed by somebody. It is a good deal to get as far as to feel that. The book will contain something like a hundred pages and will be called *The Tavern and the Night Before*. You see I was bound to wring the "tavern" in somehow, and I think I have done it fairly well. In fact, if the publishers, and then the public, are as well satisfied with the contents as I am with the title, there will be no further trouble with this first venture. But that is out of the question, I suppose. . . .

TO HARRY DE FOREST SMITH

Gardiner
May 13, 1896

I must ask you once more not to think that I have forgotten you because I have not written. This spring has been a long, queer season with me and I am glad that it is gone, though I am aware that such a feeling is hardly in accordance with what I try to believe are my honest views of life. My religion seems to be a kind of optimistic desperation and the deuce only knows what will come of it. I am trying as hard as I can to get over my almost helpless dependence upon my friends, but I find it sorry work. I say to myself that I was not made to live in solitude (and my present life amounts to little more than that) but I keep on wondering if the fates are not taking care of me, after all. If it were not for the solitude that I have been through I should not now have the "dog-gone fool notions" (I like to quote Jones) that are in my head; and if it were not for those notions I should not have my present ambitions to be something big. I don't much think that these ambitions will ever be realized, for I am getting more and more to know my limitations; but for all that, I like to keep on hoping in a sort of blind way, even if I have to stop every now and then to consider how my life is running away from me. You don't know what it is to be twenty-six years old, and still a little child as far as a prospect of worldly independence goes. You may not be exactly free just now, yourself; but you know what you can do if you are driven to it and you know that you can do that thing well. Yesterday I had to put down a carpet, but had to stop on account of my head—which will go to show about how much I am good for when it comes to scrubbing for myself. I don't know enough to teach, and any kind of business would swamp me in a month. All I have to look forward to in the way of worldly prosperity is a distant vision of a time when I may possibly earn two or three hundred dollars a year by writing. That time, however, is very far away and I don't waste a great deal of nervous energy in thinking of it. It doesn't pay.

My first venture with the book has proved a fizzle, as I knew it would. I was so thoroughly satisfied that the stuff would be rejected, that the information hardly touched me. One peculiar thing in my make-up is that I don't seem to have any capacity for discouragement, no matter how much I may be running over at the heel. I have done a few things which I know are worth while and that is a great deal to be sure of. If printed lines are good for anything, they are bound to be picked up some time; and then, if some poor devil of a man or woman feels any better or any stronger for anything that I have said, I shall have no fault to find with the scheme or anything in it. I am inclined to be a trifle solemn in my verses, but I intend that there shall always be at least a suggestion of something wiser than hatred and something better than despair.

All this, no doubt, will make you grin, but I assure you that I am getting to be pretty much in earnest. As far as common pleasure goes—the kind that makes people laugh, I mean—I don't see any more of it in the future than there has been in the twenty odd years that are behind me. My fun has got to be of another sort, though I hope, for your sake, that it won't always be in the writing of letters like this. A man has no right to wreak himself on a friend in any such wholesale way, and I'll try not to do it again.

TO HARRY DE FOREST SMITH

Gardiner
November 6, 1896

. . . For some reason I have never yet acknowledged the receipt of the postage stamps which you have been good enough to send me at various times. I am always glad to get them, for the things have a fascination for me and I think they always will. Sometimes I wonder if my interest in certain trifles will be a help or a hindrance to my ambitions. You think it will be a help, but I am not so sure of it. After reading Browning's "Rabbi Ben Ezra," postage stamps are not very powerful things to consider. They are so obviously material and my ideas are getting to be so thoroughly ideal, that the collecting of anything but wisdom often seems like going back into ignorance and barbarism. Carlyle has given me a brush lately, and I am just beginning to see what he was driving at in his *Sartor Resartus*. If the book is anything it is a denial of the existence of matter as anything but a manifestation of thought. Christianity is the same thing, and so is illuminated commonsense. I made a materialistic jab at Mrs. Eddy not long ago and saw Jones twist his eyebrows. Then he asked me to read the book, and I did so to find myself astonished and at times amused. Mrs. Eddy has wheels, but they are turning in the right direction, though some must inevitably fly off. Epictetus and Socrates, Emerson and Carlyle, Paul and Christ (or Jesus, if you prefer) tell pretty much the same story from a more general point of view. This line of thought took hold of me when I was at Harvard, but my meeting with Jones was the first thing that set it fairly going. I do not agree with Jones in his theory of the immediate practicability of advanced ideas, nor do I believe in Christian Science as anything apart from the spiritual wisdom that is latent in us all; but I do believe in idealism as the one logical and satisfactory interpretation of life, and I am quite willing to give credit to Mr. Jones and Mrs. Eddy for some valuable suggestions. . . .

TO HARRY DE FOREST SMITH

Gardiner
December 7, 1896

Things have been going so like the devil with me for the past two months that nothing short of idealism would have kept me together; and a fortnight ago, to put a finishing touch to the whole business, my mother died of diphtheria. I am not going to say very much about it, because I do not believe in that sort of thing; and most of all because it would not do any good. She has gone ahead and I am glad for her. You see I have come to look on death as a deliverance and an advancement (*vide* "Kosmos," "Two Sonnets," etc.) and I am very glad to be able to stand up and say that I am an idealist. Perhaps idealism is the philosophy of desperation, but I do not think so. To me it is the only logical and satisfactory theory of life. It is a great mystery to me that you can call *Sartor Resartus* a great book when you read it from a material point of view, but I am not keen to quarrel with you. I think too much of your friendship to run the risk of arousing any possible feeling by starting a useless argument,— so you may think "as you damn' please" and I'll do the same. As for Emerson's Essay on "Compensation," I fancy I shall get a great deal more out of it when I read it again, and that is what I intend to do very soon.

I gave Jones a copy of that most remarkable book of poems entitled *The Torrent and the Night Before,* and he professes to like it pretty well. I do not make much account of the criticism of friends—that is, their friendly criticism—but of course it is pleasant to feel that they are sincere. So I was glad to have Jones tell me that he found himself "stuck" in "The Night Before." "Nobody can read that," he said, "but yourself, and dog-gone (J. has a copyright on that) if I believe you can."—I was a little surprised at this, as I always supposed the poem was as plain as a man's nose; but I rather think the metre was what mixed it up. Metre is something he knows nothing about.

Speaking of the book, I received the whole thing (312 copies) the other morning, but did not take enough interest in them to open the package until evening. In fact, I feel as if I should like to kick them from here to Augusta and never see them again. They looked so small and so devilish blue to me that they made me sick; but now I am feeling better and am beginning to foster my same old ridiculous notion that they may amount to something some day. . . .

TO HARRY DE FOREST SMITH

Gardiner
February 3, 1897

I am sorry to see you go back on your own good judgment, but as I know your last letter was nothing but the result of a temporary enthusiasm, I have not lost any faith in your solidity of criticism and intellect. It is not in the scheme of reason, if I may say it, that you or any other man should care for everything in the book, so don't lose yourself again but keep within bounds. In the meantime I fully appreciate the very friendly spirit in which your enthusiastic screed of January 5 was scratched off and assure [you] that I haven't a particle of doubt but that you are quite honest in your general appreciation of the verses I have written. Only, don't lay it on too thick. The mere fact that so many are relatively indifferent to the merits of the book is enough to prove that it cannot carry the weight of praise you would heap upon it. There is a man in Denver who has a kind of unconscious numerical sympathy with you in your estimate of my importance, but it is very clear to me that you are both all wrong.

The *Bookman* evidently takes me for a yelling pessimist, and that I must say that I am very much surprised. And the *Bookman* is not alone, either. The same man in Denver, Colorado, thinks I have blue devils, but I assure you I have not. I also make free to say that many of my verses [were] written with a conscious hope that they might make some despairing devil a little stronger and a little better satisfied with things—not as they are, but as they are to be. This is the point the critics will not see. Because I don't dance on [an] illuminated hilltop and sing about the bobolinks and bumble-bees, they tell me that my world is a "prison house, etc." Well, if the work is good for anything, and some good men seem to think it is, I am confident that all this will be corrected some day and that people will begin to see what I am driving at. Of course "The Night Before" is purely objective, and may be called anything from pessimism to rot. I must confess that I haven't the slightest idea whether it is good for anything or not. I printed it to find out; but the opinions I have received are so conflicting that I am not much better off than I was before. . . .

TO HARRY DE FOREST SMITH

Gardiner
March 15, 1897

How long do you think a man can live in hell? I think he can live there a good many years—a hundred, perhaps, if his bowels keep in decent order—but he isn't going to have a very good time. No man can have a very good time—of the right sort, at any rate—until he understands things; and how the devil is a man to understand things in an age like this, when the whole trend of popular thought is in the wrong direction—not only that, but proud of the way it is taking? The age is all right, material progress is all right, Herbert Spencer is all right, hell is all right. These things are temporal necessities, but they are damned uninteresting to one who can get a glimpse of the real light through the clouds of time. It is that glimpse that makes me wish to live and see it out. If it were not for that glimpse, I should be tempted, as Tennyson used to be, to stick my nose into a rag soaked with chloroform and be done with it—that is, if I could screw up the courage. But now, thank God, that is not the kind of courage I am praying for; what I am after is the courage to see and to believe that my present life is the best thing for me, and that every man has it in his power to overcome whatever obstacles may be in his way—even that seeming obstacle we call by the name of Death. I have not said much about my life for the past three years—I mean the past ten—because with all its lack of anything like material hope and pleasure —it was tolerable. For all my long lean face, I never gave up; and I never shall give up. I can't do it; but I can suffer like damnation, which shows there is something wrong with me somewhere. The past three months of my life, however, are quite another thing. If they had come two years ago, or even one, I think they would have finished me. The book has helped me out a little—in fact, I was rather bewildered by its reception—but that counts (the praise, I mean) for very little. There are things here at home that are pulling me back, and I've got to look out for them. I can't get away, just now—I don't see how I can for a year—and the result is that all my best strength is required in keeping my thoughts in some sort of rational order. The one great pleasure of my life is the knowledge that my poor mother is out of it. I can't quite understand—yet—the laws of compensation that make a woman suffer what she did and from so many causes. We say she died of diphtheria. What does that mean? It means just this: she had endured all [she] could and was ready to die. I had been watching it for a year. If she had not had diphtheria, or membranous croup, or whatever it was that took her off so hellishly, she would have gone crazy. I am not going crazy, for I see some things she did not see—some things she could not see; but I am going to lose all those pleasures which are said to make up the happiness of this life and I'm glad of it. I'm glad to say that I am strong enough to do without them. There is a pleasure—a joy—that is greater than all these little selfish notions and I have found the way to it through idealism. Once I thought I was in a way to be a Christian Scientist, but that will be impossible. The system is too dependent on unsubstantial inferences. As it is taught and managed it is not Christianity, though the claim is that the two terms are synonymous. It is rapidly developing into a sect, and one that will have a tremendous power in the world; but it is only a stepping stone to the truth. It has proved the power, however, of even a partial recognition, and thereby proved the utter fallacy of all existing notions of religion—popular notions, I mean.

The great scholars of the world are for the most part spiritual imbeciles, and there is where the trouble lies. The willingness "to be a child again" comes hard—so hard that it will never come to many who are in the world today. That is not what they are here for. "The world was made in order, and the atoms march in time." It is a damned queer time to us who are here now; but it is all right and we are all going to hear it as it is—when the mortal wax gets out of our ears. . . .

TO HARRY DE FOREST SMITH

Gardiner
November 1, 1897

I was rather surprised to learn that you had been to Boston and New York, but I suppose you have the right to go where you choose. I am going over the same ground myself before long but cannot say just when. Probably I shall leave here about the tenth of this month. Sometimes I feel a little queer about going, but I know it is the only thing for me to do. I have lived this kind of life about as long as I can and my system—physical, intellectual, and spiritual—demands a change. Everything may go to pot but I don't believe it. I have an incurable feeling that I am going to do something though I never expect to make much money. If I make a living after a couple of years of brain shrivelling I shall feel that I am doing well. From the *Children* I do not expect much, if anything, in the way of direct remuneration but I shall always feel, even if I starve to death someday, that the book has done a good deal for me. Perhaps the knowledge that I have done a good deal for the book has something to do with this feeling. When I think of the hours I have spent over some of the lines in it I wonder if it is all worth while; but in the end I cease wondering. If anything is worthy of a man's best and hardest effort, that thing is the utterance of what he believes to be the truth. Of course I like a joke, and I like art for its own sake; but those things in themselves are not enough. Just as deliberate pathos in literature—that is, pathos for "effect" alone— is almost always a mistake, so, I think, is mere objectivity (I'd use some other word if I could think of it) at the best unsatisfactory. So I hope you will like my "Octaves," "Calvary," "L'Envoi," etc. better than "The Night Before." . . .

TO DANIEL GREGORY MASON

1716 Cambridge St.
27 August, 1899

. . . The principal thing I have to tell you is that I am reading Emerson's *Conduct of Life* for the first time. I confess this with burning shame, but that is not enough. It should be read by everybody before they look at so much as the title page of the *Essays,* whatever chronology may have to say. In the essay on

"Power" he takes one over his paternal knee and wallops one with a big New England shingle for about three-quarters of a New England hour. He really gets after one: "A day is a more magnificent cloth than any muslin, the mechanism that makes it is infinitely cunninger, and you shall not cancel the sleezy, fraud-ulent, rotten hours you have slipped into the piece; nor fear that any honest thread, on straighter steel or more inflexible shaft will not testify in the web." This is not exactly original, but coming as it does at the end of the whole thing it does admirable work. —If you will read this book carefully you will get changed ideas of Emerson's humanity and humor. I am ready to confess, how-ever, that the human note has a faint suggestion of falsetto here and there, but, on the other hand, may not that suggestion be the product of my own diabolical system rather than of Emerson's idealism? . . .

TO DANIEL GREGORY MASON

71 Irving Place
18 April, 1900

On the evening of the Eighteenth day of April, in the year of our Lord One Thousand Nine Hundred, I feel impelled to give you the dregs of my creative intelligence and to say that I am, as usual, a howling optimist. I am particularly optimistic just now because I am on the home stretch with *The Pauper*. It gags me to look at the twelve-hundred odd lines that have come back from the machine, but I have a satisfying consciousness of having done something and that's what makes me an optimist. By the time the thing has come back from six or seven publishers, I may be more rational, but for the present it pleases me to give myself a place among the possibilities. . . . I am glad to know that Moody has written another poem but I am sorry that he calls it an ode. That, however, is his business, not mine. I am keeping an eye out for the next *Atlantic,* and am wondering what the deuce the thing is like; for I could no more get together a poem on the Philippines than I could write a description of the human brain. All I know about the human brain is that it seems to be indispensable and that it gets to be damnably tired; and this is more than I know about the right of our incomparable republic to make a game preserve of the Philippines. My knowledge of politics is meagre and my knowledge of Destiny is so small that it doesn't count. I have to content myself with a jew's-harp and a bass-drum and let the other fellow blow the trumpets. I have a prophetic feeling that Moody has sounded a clear note—partly on account of your word "magnificent" and partly on account of a way the man has of making laddered music spring skyward from prophets' pillows and other kinds of music do things in a way on which he seems to have the God-given bulge, so to speak. . . .

TO HARRY DE FOREST SMITH

71 Irving Place
New York
June 2, 1900

. . . If the stuff that I have written is good for anything, if it is as good as some rather intelligent people seem to think, it is merely in a long trance from which it will get up some day to do a small saraband in the public place. I don't think it will ever make a big noise or a big show, but I don't, on the other hand, think it is entirely dead. As for this new book, which is a rather particular kind of twentieth century comedy, I have nothing to say except that I did it as well as I could and that I am not altogether displeased with it. I can see how it will repel a good many delicate readers, but I don't see [how] it can fail to make them a little more sensible in their attitude toward the sentimental of life and death [*sic*]—and, incidentally, of funerals. I am half inclined to think that the whole thing was suggested, indirectly enough, as you will see when you read it, by the alarming pageant on the day when E. R. Protheroe was "carried to his final resting place"—and I am sure that you will see that I am talking now about the principle of the thing, not about Protheroe: there is not so much as the ghost of him in the poem, but I fear there is rather more of old Mr. Louis (you have heard me speak of him) than I first intended there should be. There is not very much of myself, but there are pages of what certain people take to be myself: it is to these people, in fact, that I ought to dedicate the book, for they are responsible for its existence. I should never have written it, as it stands, if I had not passed through those six months of hell in the College Office; and I should never have written it at all if I had not got out of that same hell at about the time I did. . . .

TO JOSEPHINE PRESTON PEABODY

29 East 22d Street
New York City
April 12th (I think), 1901

I have just sent a thousand lines of Imperishable Stuff to the typewriter and I feel a good deal better. Four hundred lines of it are about two old men and a small boy, and the other six hundred are a woman who promised her dying spouse that she would never repeat the ceremony and six years after pledged herself to a fellow who kept a queer sort of journal and went to sleep on the day of his wife's funeral. I don't know just how people will like this sort of thing, but I shall be interested to find out. I shall send the clergyman thing along in a day or two and by that time I shall feel that I have a book pretty well in hand. . . .

TO DANIEL GREGORY MASON

450 West 23d Street
26 September, 1901

. . . It is good to know that the A.P. has brains enough to
send Moody's book into a second edition. When I received your
word to that effect I was tempted to write to him at once and
beg him to take out "by God's ring-finger stirred"—which is,
with all respect to genius, really damnable. It is so bad, in fact,
that only a genius could do it; and I am rather sorry now that
I did not write, if only for the piety of the performance. From
the twenty or so who have spoken to me of the book I have heard
nothing but praise with a big P. All, however, make an exception
of "The Menagerie"—not because they do not like it in itself
but because it seems to be hopelessly out of place. I have a notion that I shall agree with them by and by, but the thing is so
confoundedly clever that I hate to see it go. I still cling to my
first belief that "The Daguerreotype" and "The Departure" reach
the finest and highest quality of anything in the book.—There
are a few faint possibilities coming up on my own horizon, but I
do not say anything about them at present. *C.C.* has been turned
down by five houses, but he is still on the march. His trousers
are pretty badly frayed, and his general appearance seems to be
more and more disreputable on each return; but perhaps that is
all right. He is a sort of disreputable cuss, anyhow, as you
know. . . .

NOTES

NOTES

EARLY POEMS: From *The Torrent and The Night Before* and *The Children of the Night*

THE TORRENT

The first poem in Robinson's first book, *The Torrent and The Night Before* (1896); reprinted in *The Children of the Night* (1897 and 1905), *Sonnets* (1928), *Collected Poems* (1921), and subsequent collected editions.

AARON STARK

A poem which is, perhaps, a consequence of Robinson's careful reading of Molière. Published in *The Torrent and The Night Before* (1896); reprinted in *The Children of the Night* (1897 and 1905), *Sonnets* (1928), *Collected Poems* (1921), and subsequent collected editions.

THE DEAD VILLAGE

Not included in Robinson's original manuscript of his first book, called *The Tavern and The Night Before,* but added, with "Verlaine," before the publication of *The Torrent and The Night Before* (1896); reprinted in *The Children of the Night* (1897 and 1905), *Sonnets* (1928), *Collected Poems* (1921), and subsequent collected editions.

BALLADE OF A SHIP

Entitled "Ballade of the White Ship" when published in *The Harvard Advocate,* LII (October 16, 1891), 22, shortly after Robinson began his studies at Harvard College as a "special student"; reprinted in *The Torrent and The Night Before* (1896), and again under the present title in *The Children of the Night* (1897 and 1905). Excluded from *Collected Poems* (1921) and other collected editions.

The "Ship" is the white ship of an English crown prince, the son of King Henry I, which sank on November 25, 1120, while proceeding from France to England. Dante Gabriel Rossetti wrote a ballad, "The White Ship," on the same theme.

DEAR FRIENDS
    Published in *The Torrent and The Night Before* (1896); reprinted in *The Children of the Night* (1987 and 1905), *Sonnets* (1928), *Collected Poems* (1921), and subsequent collected editions.

SONNET ("When we can all so excellently give")
    Published in *The Torrent and The Night Before* (1896); reprinted in *The Children of the Night* (1897 and 1905), *Sonnets* (1928), *Collected Poems* (1921), and subsequent collected editions.

HER EYES
    Published in *The Torrent and The Night Before* (1896); reprinted in *The Children of the Night* (1897 and 1905), *Collected Poems* (1921), and subsequent collected editions.

SONNET ("The master and the slave go hand in hand")
    Published in *The Torrent and The Night Before* (1896); reprinted in *The Children of the Night* (1897 and 1905), *Sonnets* (1928), *Collected Poems* (1921), and subsequent collected editions.

ZOLA
    Published in *The Torrent and The Night Before* (1896); reprinted in *The Children of the Night* (1897 and 1905), *Sonnets* (1928), *Collected Poems* (1921), and subsequent collected editions.

BALLADE OF BROKEN FLUTES
    Entitled simply "Ballade" in *The Torrent and The Night Before* (1896); reprinted in *The Children of the Night* (1897 and 1905), *Collected Poems* (1921), and other collected editions.
    Dedicated to Alanson Schumann, a homeopathic doctor, a poet with some skill in the complex French verse forms, and Robinson's friend in Gardiner.

FOR SOME POEMS BY MATTHEW ARNOLD
    Published in *The Torrent and The Night Before* (1896); reprinted in *The Children of the Night* (1897 and 1905). Excluded from *Collected Poems* (1921) and other collected editions.

GEORGE CRABBE
    Published in *The Torrent and The Night Before* (1896); reprinted in *The Children of the Night* (1897 and 1905), *Sonnets* (1928), *Collected Poems* (1921), and subsequent collected editions.

SONNET ("Oh for a poet—for a beacon bright")

Published in the New York periodical *The Critic,* XXII (November 24, 1894), 354; reprinted in *The Torrent and The Night Before* (1896), *The Children of the Night* (1897 and 1905), *Sonnets* (1928), *Collected Poems* (1921), and subsequent collected editions.

THE ALTAR

Published in *The Torrent and The Night Before* (1896); reprinted in *The Children of the Night* (1897 and 1905), *Sonnets* (1928), *Collected Poems* (1921), and subsequent collected editions.

THE HOUSE ON THE HILL

Published in the New York periodical, *The Globe,* IV (September, 1894), 828, where the second and third stanzas ran:

> Malign them as we may
>   We cannot do them ill.
> They are all gone away.
>
> Are we more fit than they
>   To meet the Master's will?
> There is nothing more to say.

Reprinted with major textual changes in *The Torrent and the Night Before* (1896), and again in *The Children of the Night* (1897 and 1905), *Collected Poems* (1921), and subsequent collected editions.

THE WILDERNESS

Published in *The Torrent and The Night Before* (1896); reprinted in *The Children of the Night* (1897 and 1905), *Collected Poems* (1921), and subsequent collected editions.

LUKE HAVERGAL

Published in *The Torrent and The Night Before* (1896); reprinted in *The Children of the Night* (1897 and 1905), *Collected Poems* (1921), and subsequent collected editions.

THE CHORUS OF OLD MEN IN "AEGEUS"

Published in *The Torrent and The Night Before* (1896); reprinted in *The Children of the Night* (1897 and 1905), *Collected Poems* (1921), and subsequent collected editions.

There is much evidence of Robinson's early interest in classical materials. He collaborated with his friend Harry de Forest Smith, the classicist, in preparing a metrical version of Sophocles' *Antigone,* a translation which was never published, though it consumed much of

Robinson's time and energy in 1894 and 1895. The "Chorus" is not a translation, but Robinson's own comment in the Greek spirit on the legendary fate of King Aegeus, the subject of lost dramas by Sophocles and Euripides.

THE MIRACLE

Published in the New York periodical *The Globe*, IV (September, 1894), 829; reprinted in *The Torrent and The Night Before* (1896), and in *The Children of the Night* (1897 and 1905). Excluded from *Collected Poems* (1921) and other collected editions.

HORACE TO LEUCONOË

Published in *The Torrent and The Night Before* (1896); reprinted in *The Children of the Night* (1897 and 1905), *Collected Poems* (1921), and subsequent collected editions.

Robinson had completed his sonnet version of Horace's verses to Leuconoë as early as May 21, 1891, when he enclosed it in a letter to Harry Smith. Earlier, in 1890, he published a blank-verse translation of the galley race in Book V of the Aeneid in the *Reporter-Monthly* (Gardiner, Me.), May 31, p.[3], but he did not reprint it.

BALLADE OF DEAD FRIENDS

Published in *The Torrent and The Night Before* (1896); reprinted in *The Children of the Night* (1897 and 1905). Excluded from *Collected Poems* (1921) and other collected editions.

VILLANELLE OF CHANGE

Published in *The Harvard Advocate*, LII (November 25, 1891), 73; reprinted in *The Torrent and The Night Before* (1896), *The Children of the Night* (1897 and 1905), *Collected Poems* (1921), and subsequent collected editions.

THOMAS HOOD

Published in the New York periodical *The Globe*, VI (February, 1896), 91, though the poem had been submitted earlier (1891) to *The Harvard Monthly*, which had rejected it; reprinted in *The Torrent and The Night Before* (1896), *The Children of the Night* (1897 and 1905), *Sonnets* (1928), *Collected Poems* (1921), and subsequent collected editions.

FOR A BOOK BY THOMAS HARDY

Published in the New York periodical *The Critic*, XXIV (November 23, 1895), 348; reprinted in *The Torrent and The Night Before* (1896) and *The Children of the Night* (1897 and 1905). Excluded from *Collected Poems* (1921) and other collected editions.

The editors of *The Critic* added this note when the poem appeared:

"Written before the appearance of *Hearts Insurgent* [the title of *Jude the Obscure* in *Harper's Magazine*]."

SUPREMACY

Published in *The Harvard Advocate,* LIII (June 16, 1892), 122; reprinted in *The Torrent and The Night Before* (1896), *The Children of the Night* (1897 and 1905), *Sonnets* (1928), *Collected Poems* (1921), and subsequent collected editions.

THREE QUATRAINS

Published in *The Torrent and The Night Before* (1896); reprinted in *The Children of the Night* (1897 and 1905), *Collected Poems* (1921), and subsequent collected editions.

FOR CALDERON

Published only in *The Torrent and The Night Before* (1896).

JOHN EVERELDOWN

Published in *The Torrent and The Night Before* (1896); reprinted in *The Children of the Night* (1897 and 1905), *Collected Poems* (1921), and subsequent collected editions.
Robinson's first reference to "Tilbury Town" is associated with this poem; it appears in a letter to Harry Smith written on December 14, 1895. See p. 209.

THE WORLD

Published in *The Torrent and The Night Before* (1896); reprinted in *The Children of the Night* (1897 and 1905). Excluded from *Collected Poems* (1921) and other collected editions.

CREDO

Published in *The Torrent and The Night Before* (1896); reprinted in *The Children of the Night* (1897 and 1905), *Sonnets* (1928), *Collected Poems* (1921), and subsequent collected editions.

THE CHILDREN OF THE NIGHT

Published in the *Boston Evening Transcript,* January 4, 1896, p. 2; reprinted in *The Torrent and The Night Before* (1896) and as the first poem in *The Children of the Night* (1897 and 1905). Excluded from *Collected Poems* (1921) and other collected editions.

THE CLERKS

Published in the *Boston Evening Transcript,* June 4, 1896, p. 6; reprinted in *The Torrent and The Night Before* (1896), *The Children of the Night* (1897 and 1905), *Sonnets* (1928), *Collected Poems* (1921), and subsequent collected editions.

BALLADE BY THE FIRE
  Published in *The Torrent and The Night Before* (1896); reprinted in *The Children of the Night* (1897 and 1905), *Collected Poems* (1921), and subsequent collected editions.

ON THE NIGHT OF A FRIEND'S WEDDING
  Published in *The Torrent and The Night Before* (1896); reprinted in *The Children of the Night* (1897 and 1905), *Sonnets* (1928), *Collected Poems* (1921), and subsequent collected editions.

VERLAINE
  Published in the *Boston Evening Transcript,* July 28, 1896, p. 7; reprinted in *The Torrent and The Night Before* (1896), *The Children of the Night* (1897 and 1905), *Sonnets* (1928), *Collected Poems* (1921), and subsequent collected editions.

THE GARDEN
  Entitled "God's Garden" in the New York periodical *The Globe,* VI (September, 1896), 30; reprinted with the present title in *The Torrent and The Night Before* (1896), *The Children of the Night* (1896 and 1905), *Sonnets* (1928), *Collected Poems* (1921), and subsequent collected editions.

TWO SONNETS ("Just as I wonder at the twofold screen")
    ("Never until our souls are strong enough")
  Published in *The Torrent and The Night Before* (1896); reprinted in *The Children of the Night* (1897 and 1905), *Sonnets* (1928), *Collected Poems* (1921), and subsequent collected editions.

WALT WHITMAN
  Published in *The Torrent and The Night Before* (1896); reprinted in *The Children of the Night* (1897 and 1905). Excluded from *Collected Poems* (1921) and subsequent collected editions.

KOSMOS
  Published in the New York periodical *The Globe,* V (October, 1895), 407; reprinted in *The Torrent and The Night Before* (1896) and *The Children of the Night* (1897 and 1905). Excluded from *Collected Poems* (1921) and subsequent collected editions.

AN OLD STORY
  Published in *The Torrent and The Night Before* (1896); reprinted in *The Children of the Night* (1897 and 1905), *Collected Poems* (1921), and subsequent collected editions.

A POEM FOR MAX NORDAU

Published only in *The Torrent and The Night Before* (1896).

Max Nordau (1848-1923) was the Hungarian doctor of medicine who wrote *Entartung,* translated into English in 1895 with the title *Degeneration.* Robinson felt that his readers failed to appreciate the humor of the poem, and this is one of his reasons, certainly, for not reprinting it.

BOSTON

Published in the *Boston Evening Transcript,* October 8, 1896, p. 6; reprinted in *The Torrent and The Night Before* (1896) and *The Children of the Night* (1897). Only the octave of the sonnet appears in Scribner's edition of *The Children of the Night* (1905), and the octave has been reprinted in *Collected Poems* (1921) and subsequent collected editions.

THE NIGHT BEFORE

The concluding poem in Robinson's first volume, *The Torrent and The Night Before* (1896); reprinted in *The Children of the Night* (1896 and 1905). Excluded from *Collected Poems* (1921) and subsequent collected editions.

This statement appears below the title of the poem in 1896: "As if God made him and then wondered why."

TWO MEN

Published in *The Children of the Night* (1897 and 1905); reprinted in *Collected Poems* (1921) and subsequent collected editions.

RICHARD CORY

Published in *The Children of the Night* (1897 and 1905); reprinted in *Collected Poems* (1921) and subsequent collected editions.

TWO OCTAVES

Published only in *The Children of the Night* (1897 and 1905).

CALVARY

Published in *The Children of the Night* (1897 and 1905); reprinted in *Sonnets* (1928), *Collected Poems* (1921), and subsequent collected editions.

THE STORY OF THE ASHES AND THE FLAME

Published in *The Children of the Night* (1897 and 1905); reprinted in *Sonnets* (1928), *Collected Poems* (1921), and subsequent collected editions.

AMARYLLIS

   Published in the *Boston Evening Transcript,* August 2, p. 6; reprinted in *The Children of the Night* (1897 and 1905), *Sonnets* (1928), *Collected Poems* (1921), and subsequent collected editions.
   Amaryllis is the name of a shepherdess in poems by Vergil and Theocritus; it is a conventional name in pastoral poetry.

CLIFF KLINGENHAGEN

   Published in *The Children of the Night* (1897 and 1905); reprinted in *Sonnets* (1928), *Collected Poems* (1921), and subsequent collected editions.

CHARLES CARVILLE'S EYES

   Published in *The Children of the Night* (1897 and 1905); reprinted in *Sonnets* (1928), *Collected Poems* (1921), and subsequent collected editions.

FLEMING HELPHENSTINE

   Published in *The Children of the Night* (1897 and 1905); reprinted in *Sonnets* (1928), *Collected Poems* (1921), and subsequent collected editions.

REUBEN BRIGHT

   Published in *The Children of the Night* (1897 and 1905); reprinted in *Sonnets* (1928), *Collected Poems* (1921), and subsequent collected editions.

THE TAVERN

   Published in *The Children of the Night* (1897 and 1905); reprinted in *Sonnets* (1928), *Collected Poems* (1921), and subsequent collected editions.

OCTAVES

   Octave V appeared in the New York periodical *The Globe,* VII (June, 1897), 179; reprinted and grouped with new octaves in *The Children of the Night* (1897 and 1905). Octaves I and III excluded from *Collected Poems* (1921) and subsequent collected editions, in which the remaining twenty-three octaves have been renumbered.

TWO QUATRAINS

   Published in *The Children of the Night* (1897 and 1905); reprinted in *Collected Poems* (1921) and subsequent collected editions.

ROMANCE

   Published only in *The Children of the Night* (1897 and 1905).

L'ENVOI

Published in *The Children of the Night* (1897 and 1905); reprinted in *Sonnets* (1928), *Collected Poems* (1921), and subsequent collected editions.

CAPTAIN CRAIG

Published in *Captain Craig* (1902); reprinted in *Captain Craig* (1915), an edition with additional poems; cut drastically, revised, and reprinted in *Collected Poems* (1921) and subsequent editions.

The first title for the poem was "The Pauper," but it gave way to "Captain Craig" before the poem was sent off to Scribner's for a reading in early May, 1900.

Captain Craig, the main character of the poem, is to some extent a portrait of Alfred Louis, an impoverished intellectual with great knowledge, apparently, of politics, religion, and literature and many acquaintances among distinguished men and women in England and America. Robinson met Louis during his first period of residence in New York, from late 1897 to May, 1898.

The members of the "Chrysalis" group resemble Robinson's friends in Gardiner: Arthur Blair, a banker and an amateur violinist; Linville Robbins, a geologist; and Seth Pope, a teacher, who often joined the poet in social evenings in a back room above a store in Gardiner during the spring of 1897. The four friends called their informal group "The Quadruped."

The use of the band in "Captain Craig" was undoubtedly suggested by the elaborate funeral for a Gardiner music teacher, E. R. Protheroe, which Robinson had observed. Its crowning feature was a funeral procession led by the Gardiner brass band and enlivened by the Knights of Pythias in full regalia.

ISAAC AND ARCHIBALD

Published in *Captain Craig* (1902); reprinted in *Captain Craig* (1915), *Collected Poems* (1921), and subsequent collected editions.

248. "Stafford's Cabin" is the title of a short narrative poem in *The Man Against the Sky*.

THE RETURN OF MORGAN AND FINGAL

Published in *Captain Craig* (1902); reprinted in *Captain Craig* (1915), *Collected Poems* (1921), and subsequent collected editions.

AUNT IMOGEN

Published in *Captain Craig* (1902); reprinted in *Captain Craig* (1915), *Collected Poems* (1921), and subsequent collected editions.

The first title for the poem was "The Old Maid."

"Aunt Imogen" had its source in Robinson's affectionate relationships with the wife of his brother Herman, Emma, and her three little girls.

THE KLONDIKE

Published in *Captain Craig* (1902); reprinted in *Captain Craig* (1915), *Collected Poems* (1921), and subsequent collected editions.

THE GROWTH OF "LORRAINE"

Published in *Captain Craig* (1902); reprinted in *Captain Craig* (1915), *Sonnets* (1928), *Collected Poems* (1921), and subsequent collected editions.

THE SAGE

Published in *Captain Craig* (1902); reprinted in *Captain Craig* (1915), *Sonnets* (1928), *Collected Poems* (1921), and subsequent collected editions.
"The Sage" is a tribute to Ralph Waldo Emerson.

ERASMUS

Published in *The Harvard Monthly*, XXXI (December, 1900), 110; reprinted in *Captain Craig* (1902 and 1915), *Sonnets* (1928), *Collected Poems* (1921), and subsequent collected editions.

THE WOMAN AND THE WIFE

Published in *Captain Craig* (1902); reprinted in *Captain Craig* (1915), *Sonnets* (1928), *Collected Poems* (1921), and subsequent collected editions.

THE BOOK OF ANNANDALE

Published in *Captain Craig* (1902); reprinted in *Captain Craig* (1915), *Collected Poems* (1921), and subsequent collected editions.

SAINTE-NITOUCHE

Published in *Captain Craig* (1902); reprinted in *Captain Craig* (1915), *Collected Poems* (1921), and subsequent collected editions.
Professor Emery Neff has suggested that the poem is an "apparent reversal of Dimmesdale's experience in Hawthorne's novel [*The Scarlet Letter*]." See *Edwin Arlington Robinson* (New York: William Sloane Associates, Inc., 1948), p. 122.

AS A WORLD WOULD HAVE IT

Published in *Captain Craig* (1902); reprinted in *Captain Craig* (1915), *Collected Poems* (1921), and subsequent collected editions.
The action in Robinson's poem begins at a point after the conclusion of the *Alcestis* of Euripides. There Alcestis is last seen being led into the palace by a happy Admetus, who commands all Thessaly to rejoice in celebration of her miraculous return from the underworld.

THE CORRIDOR

Published in *The Harvard Monthly*, XXVII (February, 1899), 206; reprinted in *Captain Craig* (1902 and 1915), *Collected Poems* (1921), and subsequent collected editions.

CORTÈGE

Published in *Captain Craig* (1902); reprinted in *Captain Craig* (1915), *Collected Poems* (1921), and subsequent collected editions.

THE WIFE OF PALISSY

Published in *Captain Craig* (1902); reprinted in *Captain Craig* (1915); entitled "Partnership" in *Collected Poems* (1921) and in subsequent collected editions.

Bernard Palissy (1510-1589) was the famous French potter who worked for nearly sixteen years at great sacrifice to discover the secret of the manufacture of fine porcelain. Robinson probably discovered Palissy by reading Longfellow's "Keramos."

LETTERS

February 8, 1891. Harry de Forest Smith. Smith, a schoolmate of Robinson's at Gardiner High School, was the son of a ship's caulker and small farmer. Smith attended Bowdoin College and Harvard, and became a distinguished teacher of the classics at Amherst College.

March 10, 1891. *"Arena."* A monthly published in Boston from 1890-1909. B. O. Flower was the editor in 1891.

"Albert Ross." The author also of *Thou Shalt Not.*

"Sapho." Published by the French novelist, Alphonse Daudet (1840-1897) in 1884. Daudet is the author also of *Aventures prodigieuses de Tartarin de Tarascon* (1872), *Fromont jeune et Risler aîné* (1874), and *Jack* (1876).

"The Pace That Kills." Published by Edgar Saltus (1855-1921) in 1899. Other works by Saltus, known as the American Oscar Wilde, that had appeared by 1891 are *Mr. Incoul's Misadventure* (1887), *The Truth About Tristrem Varick* (1888), *Eden* (1888), *A Transaction in Hearts* (1889), *Love and Lore* (1890), as well as the essays in *The Philosophy of Disenchantment* (1885) and *The Anatomy of Negation* (1886).

"A Saint Anthony (Comstock)." Anthony Comstock (1844-1915) organized the New York Society for the Suppression of Vice in 1873 and, as the chief special agent for the society, gave himself largely to the suppression of immoral and salacious literature.

May 21, 1891, "the ode of Horace." The Eleventh Ode of Horace's First Book. See p. 18 for a later version of the poem by Robinson. "Bulwer." Bulwer-Lytton (Edward George Bulwer, 1st Baron Lytton of Knebworth, 1803-1873), English politician, novelist, dramatist, poet, and translator (*The Odes and Epodes of Horace*. Edinburgh and London: W. Blackwood and Sons, 1869).

September 13, 1891. "Frédéric César de Sumichrast." Professor of French at Harvard, editor and translator of French works, including the writings of Théophile Gautier.

December 8, 1891. "Robert Morss Eliott." Charles W. Eliot (1834-1926) was then president of Harvard and was to be until his resignation in 1909. Robert Morss Lovett, then editor-in-chief of *The Harvard Monthly*, became a professor of English at the University of Chicago.
"the *Monthly*." *The Harvard Monthly* was one of the two important undergraduate literary magazines and the one with the more prestige in Robinson's years at Harvard because of the association of Lovett, William Vaughn Moody, Philip Savage, Hugh McCulloch, and Trumbull Stickney.
"my sonnet on Hood." "Thomas Hood," p. 21.
"the *Advocate*." *The Harvard Advocate*, the other undergraduate periodical, not so exclusively literary as the *Monthly*.
"with Villanelle." "Villanelle of Change," p. 20.

April 17, 1892. "make no measure. . . ." This poem was published in the New York periodical *The Globe*, VI (May, 1896), 143-144. It is reprinted in Charles Beecher Hogan's *A Bibliography of Edwin Arlington Robinson* (New Haven: Yale University Press, 1936), p. 173.
"There is a drear and lonely tract. . . ." See "Supremacy," p. 22.

May 23, 1892. "a lecture on *Sir Gawain and the Green Knight* by Prof. Kittredge." George Lyman Kittredge (1860-1941) was a professor of English at Harvard. His interests were linguistic, literary, and historical, and he is remembered especially for his publications on Virgil, Chaucer, Shakespeare, the medieval romances, the popular ballad, and the American colonials. The Harvard University Press published *A Study of Gawain and the Green Knight* in 1916.

November 29, 1892. "Prof. Norton's lectures in 'Fine Arts.'" Charles Eliot Norton (1827-1908) was the first professor of the history of art at Harvard. He was an art critic, an editor, a translator (of *The Divine Comedy*), and a teacher of rare power.
"The Darius Inscription." The great inscription in three kinds of

cuneiform writing engraved by Darius I, king of Persia, at Behistun, describing the defeat of the usurper Gaumata and the restoration of the kingdom of the Achaemonidae. Henry (not May) Rawlinson succeeded in translating the inscription in 1846 after beginning work upon it in 1835.

"Chauncey Depew's after-dinner speeches." Chauncey Depew (1834-1928) was president and chairman of the board of directors of the New York Central and Hudson River railway, U.S. Senator from New York (1899-1911), and a public speaker of great popularity.

"World's Fair." The World's Columbian Exposition was opened at Chicago on October 21, 1892.

February 5, 1893. "broken out." shingles.

"that long siege with my ear." One of the urgent reasons for Robinson's coming to Harvard was his desire to receive periodic treatments for his ear at the Massachusetts General Hospital.

October 1, 1893. "hug my own particular phantoms." Denham Sutcliffe, in a note on this letter in *Untriangulated Stars*, p. 318, has pointed out an apparent indebtedness to Bryant's "Thanotopsis" (ll. 63-64).

> ". . . and each one as before will chase
> His favorite phantom."

February 4, 1894. "like the stone house on the hill." Hermann Hagedorn reports in *Edwin Arlington Robinson, A Biography* (New York: The Macmillan Company, 1939), pp. 47-48, that Robinson and Smith often met on Iron Mine Hill behind the Smith homestead to smoke and to talk and that they discussed building there a house of stone.

February 25, 1894. "The House on the Hill." See p. 12 for a later version of the poem.

"Cicero's first oration against Catiline." At the age of sixteen Robinson turned into blank verse a high school assignment of a translation of Cicero's first oration. Years later he recalled the lavish expenditure of time upon the variation of the caesura and other technical matters involving the music and the rhythm of the verse.

March 18, 1894. *"Many Inventions."* A collection of fourteen stories by Rudyard Kipling, with an introduction ("To the True Romance") and a concluding "Envoy" in verse. Published by D. Appleton and Company, New York, 1893.

April 22, 1894. "description of the wood-cutter and his dog." *The Task*, V, 41-57.

"Don Quixote." In Austin Dobson's *At the Sign of the Lyre* (New York: H. Holt and Company, 1885).

May 27, 1894. "The Night Before." See p. 37.

June 3, 1894. "I tell you. . . ." See p. 48. ("The Night Before," ll. 359-361).

February 3, 1895. *"The Manxman."* A novel by Hall Caine (Sir Thomas Henry Hall Caine) published by D. Appleton and Company, New York, 1895.

December 14, 1895. "that sonnet translation of Horace's ode to Leuconoë." See p. 18.
"a piece of deliberate degeneration called 'Luke Havergal.'" See p. 15.
"Old John Evereldown." See "John Evereldown," p. 26, and "The Tavern," p. 55.
"The 'Tavern' part of my book." An early title for Robinson's first volume was *The Tavern and The Night Before.* See letter to Smith written on March 7, 1896, p. 210.

May 13, 1896. "I like to quote Jones." Jones is the middle-aged Christian Scientist who encouraged Robinson to read Mary Baker Eddy's *Science and Health* and who discussed with the young poet forms of idealistic thought.

February 3, 1897. "a man in Denver." The book reviewer of the *Denver Times*.
"The *Bookman.*" Harry Thurstone Peck wrote in the section of the literary journal entitled "Chronicle and Comment": "There is true fire in his verse, and there are the swing and the singing of emotion in his lines; but his limitations are vital. His humor is of a grim sort, and the world is not beautiful to him, but a prison-house. In the night-time there is weeping and sorrow, and joy does not come in the morning. But here and there he lets himself go, and the cry of a yearning spirit enters the lute of Orpheus and sounds a sweet and wondrous note." The *Bookman,* IV (February, 1897), 510.

March 15, 1897. "My poor mother is out of it." Mary Robinson died suddenly in November, 1896, after she had returned to Gardiner from a visit to Boston.

August 27, 1899. Daniel Gregory Mason. A composer, author, lecturer, and teacher. He came from a musical family; his father, Henry Mason, was one of the founders of the Mason and Hamlin Piano Company. Daniel Gregory Mason is known widely for his books about music (*From Grieg to Brahms*, 1902; *Beethoven and His Forerunners*, 1904; *The Romantic Composers*, 1906; *Contemporary Composers*, 1918, to mention a few titles among many), though his own musical compositions include three symphonies and much chamber music. From 1929 to 1938 he was the MacDowell Professor of Music at Columbia University. Friendship with William Vaughn Moody began during Mason's undergraduate years at Harvard (1891-1895). Mason and Robinson became friends later, in 1899, during Robinson's uncomfortable tour of duty in President Eliot's office.

"A day is a more magnificent cloth. . . ." In Emerson's "Power," *Conduct of Life* (*Complete Works,* Riverside Edition, Cambridge, Mass., 1883, VI), p. 81.

April 18, 1900. *"The Pauper."* The original title of "Captain Craig." See note on "Captain Craig," p. 231.

"Moody has written another poem." "An Ode in Time of Hesitation," *The Atlantic Monthly,* LXXXV (May, 1900), 593-598.

June 2, 1900. "As for this new book." *The Pauper* or *Captain Craig.*
"E. R. Protheroe." See note on "Captain Craig," p. 231.
"old Mr. Louis." See note on "Captain Craig," p. 231.
"six months of hell in the College Office." Robinson was employed as a confidential clerk for President Eliot of Harvard from January to June, 1899. The poet found his work in University 5 to be routine and uncongenial, and he thought that his verse suffered. In October, 1899, Robinson went to live in New York, settling at 71 Irving Place.

April 12, 1901. Josephine Preston Peabody. Miss Peabody (1874-1922) was a poet and a playwright. Her volumes of poetry include *The Wayfarers* (1898), *The Singing Leaves* (1913), and *Harvest Moon* (1916). *Fortune and Men's Eyes* (1900), *Marlowe* (1901), *The Piper* (1909), and *The Wolf of Gubbio* are the titles of some of her plays. In 1906 Miss Peabody married Lionel Simeon Marks of the Engineering Department at Harvard University. Robinson's letters to Miss Peabody have especial value for his frank, tactful, and detailed criticism of her verse.

"Four hundred lines of it are about two old men and a small boy." "Isaac and Archibald," p. 124.
"the other six hundred. . . ." "The Book of Annandale," p. 150.
"the clergyman thing." "Sainte-Nitouche," p. 166.

September 26, 1901. "A.P." American Public.
"by God's ring-finger stirred." In "An Ode in Time of Hesitation," *Poems* (Boston and New York: Houghton, Mifflin and Company, 1901), p. 16. The pertinent lines in the poem are:

> And lo, the shard the potter cast away
> Was grown a fiery chalice crystal-fine
> Fulfilled of the divine
> Great wine of battle wrath by God's ring-finger stirred.

"The Menagerie," *Poems,* p. 55.
"The Daguerreotype," *Poems*, p. 98.
"The Departure," *Poems*, p. 72.